FINDING FORWARD

FINDING FORWARD

VERONICA ALLAM

PALMETTO
PUBLISHING
Charleston, SC
www.PalmettoPublishing.com

Copyright © 2024 by Veronica Allam

All rights reserved

No portion of this book may be reproduced, stored in a retrieval system, or transmitted in any form by any means–electronic, mechanical, photocopy, recording, or other–except for brief quotations in printed reviews, without prior permission of the author.

Paperback ISBN: 979-8-8229-3653-9

DEDICATION

Husband, what *if* I told you every moment that led to my decision to write this book? First you'd brace yourself for another one of my brilliant "what if" plans. Then you'd laugh and say, "You silly wife" or "You silly Texican." But what began as an idea to tell our story, our love story, from my perspective, shockingly turned into something much more. Unbeknownst to me, this writing became a cathartic and therapeutic process. It forced me to go back in time and to relive every raw, vulnerable, painful moment; yet it also reminded me of the beauty and love throughout the entire story. What I thought would only be a salve for you became something meant for me too. No longer is it just our love story; it's now my story and my journey leading to you. And to my surprise, by the end, it became something meant for Tristan as well.

Husband, my love, you captured my heart from the moment I met you, and you've held it tightly ever since. I wouldn't change any of it because from within the chaotic mess came our greatest joys. I'll always choose you.

My dearest Tristan, this story portrays my road to you as well. You, dear kid, are truly one of the best things I've ever done in my life. Nothing in our lives is ever an accident. Our fates are always meant for us, and God has plans for our journeys. I love you more than you'll ever know.

PROLOGUE

Two distinct and undeniable soft, yet blinding, pink vertical lines stared back at me, clear as day. One line was brighter than the other; the second line faint, but still blatantly obvious. What if I held the pregnancy stick up to the light? Maybe I'd be able to see the second pink line more clearly? Or for that matter, unsee it entirely. As if the lighting in the guest bathroom were the problem! My eyes were deceiving me, because there was no way this was happening! When I peed, did I hold the applicator too close or not far away enough? Maybe I peed on it wrong, if there was such a thing. There was no shaking the First Response pregnancy stick to move the pee around and get a more accurate reading. Maybe I picked it up and read it too soon? I let it sit longer than three minutes, hoping to undo what had already been shown. *Pregnant.*

"It's a fluke; it must be! Undoubtedly a false positive," I thought. As if any of those sad attempts and excuses would make me any less pregnant. I began to feel the weight and heaviness of this revelation as it sank into the pit of my stomach and immediately weighed me down. All at once, fear and excitement consumed every fiber of my being. Until then, a combination of these emotions had been utterly foreign to me. "Pregnant, holy shit! How did I get here? How did I let this happen? What now? What am I going to do? Where do I go from here?"

CHAPTER 1

In the summer of 1997, I was sixteen years old, and I was heading into my junior year of high school. My summer break was spent hanging out at family cookouts and socializing with my friends. We'd either end up at the local Motel 6 or at someone's house party, which consisted of pumping kegs, doing shots, and shotgunning too many cans of Budweiser or whatever alcohol was readily available. I'm sure a few fuzzy navel wine coolers were involved. The occasional escapades with my older sister, Yasmin, involved sneaking me into Dallas-area nightclubs using her driver's license as my way in, while she used a fake ID. And let's not forget the on-again, off-again high-school-boyfriend drama with Sebastian. Our fights always involved him cheating on me, so it was no surprise for me to hear recent whisperings of yet another one of Sebastian's cheating scandals with some random girl I may or may not have known. I felt confused and wanted desperately to believe that the latest rumors weren't true. So Yasmin's invitation for me to join her on a quick weekend road trip to Oklahoma City to visit Eli, her long-distance boyfriend, came at the perfect time. I didn't hesitate—I jumped at the idea.

I desperately needed and welcomed the escape from the high school drama and perpetual cycle of break-up, make-up with Sebastian. However, my joy about leaving was short-lived. Once Sebastian found out I was going away for the weekend, his jealousy set in, and he made every attempt to tag along. However, the truth was that he didn't want me to be left alone with Damian, Eli's brother, for fear that we'd "hook up." I was weak, and I buckled, agreeing to Sebastian joining us on our road trip. Plus I secretly enjoyed that he was getting a taste of his own medicine. The plans for the weekend involved staying at Tammi's place (Eli and Damian's mom). We'd be going to a local classic-car show and lowrider festival in downtown OKC. A low-key weekend is exactly what I wanted and needed.

The day I met him is hazy in my mind. However, I do recall the brief introduction made by Eli. "Vero, this is my cousin Offmed. Offmed, this is Yasmin's sister, Vero." Vero is short for Veronica and my childhood nickname.

"What an exciting name," I thought reflexively. Offmed—unlike anything I'd ever heard before. Boys in my high school had common names like Jeremy, Ben, and Mason. His name intrigued me.

I quickly learned that Eli had utterly butchered the pronunciation of his own cousin's name. Although it sounded like OFF-med, his name's real pronunciation was AH-med. Ahmed. I was now even more captivated by him.

With a brief handshake and a mutual gaze, we said hello. There was something about him, and I couldn't quite put my finger on it. It was not just that he was tall and handsome, or that the hazel color of his eyes had sucked me in; there was an enigmatic pull to him that I couldn't shake, much less explain. I tucked away my excitement and brushed off the unusual feeling because surely I was going crazy and imagining it. I didn't say anything beyond a graceful "hello."

I returned to reality, not putting any more thought into the strangeness I felt during my short encounter with Ahmed. Instead I stored the moment in my mind and spent the rest of the time in Oklahoma hanging out with Sebastian. Before I knew it, Sunday had arrived, and our trip was over. It was time to drive back to Fort Worth, and my encounter with Eli's cousin was soon a distant memory.

CHAPTER 2

I didn't see Ahmed again until the summer of 1998. God must've heard my prayers because, with the Fourth of July approaching, my second weekend trip to Oklahoma City with Yasmin was on my calendar. This time I would be going as a freshly single seventeen-year-old with no Sebastian and only one objective: have fun and enjoy myself!

The three-hour drive north from Fort Worth to Oklahoma City was always uneventful. However, the flat plains and soft rolling hills made the drive peaceful, and I got lost in my thoughts. The gas station just north of Gainesville, Texas, was the last opportunity to buy beer with higher alcohol content. Oklahoma's beer is weak at 3.2 percent. But this was not a "weak-ass beer" kind of weekend! Crossing over the infamous Red River at the Texas-Oklahoma border (yes, it is indeed red because of its red soil) indicated that we were halfway to our destination of Choctaw, Oklahoma.

Pulling into Tammi's driveway was a lovely breath of fresh air, literally and figuratively. Her five-acre lot was well-landscaped and featured a beautiful pond out front. There was a cookout at Tammi's house, which meant the place was full of people, including many of Eli and Damian's hot and single friends. As conversations echoed through the living room, I sat on Tammi's couch and sipped a red Solo cup full of some whiskey concoction Damian had thrown together for me. It was way too strong, and I quickly learned that whiskey burn is a real thing. I then felt someone staring. Not in the creepy, "hairs standing up on the back of your neck" kind of way, but it was that same weird magnetic pull again. The feeling was familiar, and as I scanned the room, I spotted him. He was taller than the last time, another year older, wearing white basketball tear-away pants with black stripes down the side and a sleeveless T-shirt. A new—well, new to me—somewhat freshly inked USMC tattoo was penned across his left deltoid muscle. It was Ahmed. His left hand was held up to his mouth, index finger stretched over his cheek, thumb underneath his chin. His hazel eyes were almost translucent from the sunlight, and those eyes were on me. With unspoken words and his failed attempt at hiding the smirk on his face, he still managed to transmit his message: I'm looking at you.

As evening approached, the gang all headed to an area in downtown Oklahoma City called Bricktown to watch the fireworks. Standing among throngs of people at an intersection, waiting for the crosswalk sign to change, I remember saying, "I don't want to get lost in the crowd."

Without missing a beat, Ahmed replied, "I'll hold your hand to cross the street."

This guy was slick, and as inconspicuous as he tried to be, he couldn't hide his charm. I hadn't even realized that he'd been standing next to me the entire time.

As our light changed, we walked ahead, hand in hand, with stupid grins on our faces. I was taken aback by how well our hands fit together. At that moment, I noticed that his unwavering posture was both poised and relaxed, and he exuded a confidence that I didn't have. His six-foot frame towered over my five-foot three figure, and I'd catch myself sneaking looks up at him. I'm not sure how long after we crossed the street it occurred to me that we were still holding hands! I didn't want to pull my hand away from his, but I knew I had to because we were reaching that awkward "holding hands for too long" moment, and people around us would surely notice. The last thing I wanted was for people to start talking, teasing, or giving us shit and making it more obvious something was happening between us. I got the sense that he didn't want to let go either, so I unclasped my hand from his first. Looking up and smiling at him, I shuffled off and caught up to my sister and Eli.

"Yasmin, Ahmed just held my hand. I think he might like me or something."

Surprised, Yasmin replied, "What?! Ahmed? Are you sure? Maybe you're reading into it all wrong?"

All Eli could muster was shaking his head back and forth, laughing and mumbling under his breath, "Good ol' Offmed!"

Upon returning to Tammi's house to call it a night, Yasmin and Eli hurried to the bedroom and shut the door, leaving me without a bed to sleep on and forcing me to sleep on the couch. Once again I didn't see him, as he was lying on the other couch next to mine. He must've picked up on how upset I was because he turned over and asked me, "Do you want a massage?"

Damn, he was *good*! Being a smooth talker suited him well. The pickup line worked—the word "sure" was rolling off my tongue before I knew it. He hurriedly came over and sat behind me on Tammi's couch, gently shifting my hair around until it pooled onto one side. His hands were firm but gentle, and my shoulders and neck welcomed the sweet release of stress and tension that had built up. However, his lips were on mine in what seemed like the blink of an eye. His lips were tender yet eager. After some first- and second-base action, we came up for air. He lay behind me on the couch, engulfed me in his arms, and held me tightly, whispering into my ear, "This is like a dream come true." Everything in me believed him. I smiled and fell fast asleep.

Waking up the following day, while still trying to process the events that had unfolded on that couch the night before, Ahmed and I jotted down our numbers, made the exchange, and off he went. I didn't see him for the remainder of my trip, but his words still lingered in my mind. I dreaded having to go back home. I didn't want my time with Ahmed to end—not yet. Yasmin and I made the familiar drive back to Fort Worth. I now had my second unforgettable memory with Ahmed.

CHAPTER 3

I'm not sure how long I was back home before I fell right back into the arms of Sebastian. The trail of destruction left in our wake was familiar, and it was normal for us. I was comfortable with the drama, and I settled on being OK with it. I concluded that this routine was the natural progression of our relationship. Sebastian was charming and convincing in his attempt to win me back again. After a bit of manipulation and gaslighting, he apologized, and I forgave him. Sebastian was charismatic, and he could charm his way out of anything. We had history, familiar friends and interests, and time invested, and we did have a lot of fun together; on paper, we were a good fit, and despite it all, I did love him. He's what many would refer to as my high school sweetheart. Being the hopeless romantic I am, I was willing to make it work. However, not without wounding his heart and ego a little in the process. I told him about Ahmed for no other reason than to make him jealous. It worked. Petty, yes, but it gave me the boost of confidence in my self-esteem that I wasn't getting otherwise.

Ahmed called me first. I loved the sound of his voice. It was deep, captivating, and assertive, and I teased him that he sounded like Barry White. He was intelligent, honest, well-spoken, had a great sense of humor, and had knowledge of the world from his travels. I was immediately enamored. From our conversations, I learned he was half Egyptian (which made his name make a lot more sense). He was in the Marine Corps, hence the USMC tattoo and the self-assuredness. Ahmed was stationed in San Angelo and had been in OKC on leave while we were there. He half-jokingly said it wasn't a far drive to Fort Worth and he wanted to come to see me. I laughed it off without taking him too seriously. In jest, I agreed to his visit, not thinking he'd follow through. Besides, we didn't make official plans, and I never even gave him my address, so he didn't know where I lived. I convinced myself he wouldn't come. Until this point, I had zero experience with what an honest and interested guy was. I had no concept of what a nice guy who stayed true to his word was—or that they even existed. "No way did he mean it! Why would he want to come to see me?" I thought. Seriously, my lack of self-worth was pathetic. However, from our conversations, talking and listening to Ahmed ignited something within my heart that I didn't know existed. A wonder, a desire, and a longing to know what being with him could be like. Silly teenage-girl daydreaming.

Saturday afternoon, sitting in Sebastian's room, I felt a vibrating at my hip—my phone was buzzing and displaying Ahmed's number. I ignored his call. My dad immediately called me and said Eli's cousin had just stopped by looking for me, and my dad had informed him I was with my boyfriend. Yasmin also called, letting me know she gave Ahmed our parents' address. In my mind, all I could think was, "He did it! He came!" His actions made my heart swell, and I smiled at the thought of him in my town.

Alluding to me having sex with Ahmed, a confused Sebastian asked, "What did you do with him that he's driving three hours here to see you?"

"We kissed; that was it." As if there needed to be more reason to have another guy interested in me. Trying to prove my love to Sebastian by not answering Ahmed's repeated calls made me feel like the worst person in the world. I regretted it immediately and felt horrible. I convinced myself it was better that way.

A couple of days passed before I spoke with Ahmed. I got the courage to call and apologize for my childish behavior. He said it was no big deal. He informed me that while driving to Fort Worth to see me, his Camaro had spun out just east of Weatherford and ended up on a grassy hill. The guilt set in even more for me, but he had a remarkable ability to diffuse an awkward situation and find the humor in all of it. I secretly loved that about him. Gradually the phone calls between Ahmed and me became less frequent, and before long, I'd heard he was living in Monterey, California for DLI school (Defense Language Institute). With this distance, I guessed there would be no seeing him again. At least not anytime soon. Once again, it was better that way, I thought, but not without Ahmed having left an impression in my heart.

January 1999: that was the date of our third encounter. Ahmed was a groomsman, and I was maid of honor at Yasmin and Eli's wedding. Standing there in his dress blues, he looked dashing as ever. I forced myself not to gawk. But there it was again, that mysterious force of attraction. I was being drawn and pulled toward Ahmed in ways I couldn't explain. He was there with a date, and, well, Sebastian was there as my date. In my mind, the simplest strategy here was to avoid and ignore Ahmed because maybe then I wouldn't feel the desire to be near him. I gave no credence to whatever I felt anytime Ahmed was nearby. But damn if I didn't want more of it.

CHAPTER 4

My senior year was memorable yet short-lived because I had graduated early in December with plans of walking the stage with my class in May of 1999. We were the last graduating class of the century, and there was something worth celebrating about that. My senior year consisted of the homecoming dance, prom, parties, weekend drinking, sleepovers with friends, and the never-ending back-and-forth with the same two-timing boyfriend, Sebastian. You'd think by then I would have learned he was no good for me. I was too forgiving, gullible, naive, and unsure of myself. Boys being unfaithful was the norm, or so I thought. With movies like *Cruel Intentions* and *She's All That*, it was no wonder I'd normalized boys tallying up their hookups and sexual conquests only to boast about them later like some "secret" badge of honor. My senior year passed quickly, and graduation came and went faster than I'd anticipated. However, I was unprepared for what would come next, just a few short months after graduation.

Rumors were swirling of my boyfriend, Sebastian, and my good friend, Audrey, making out. The extent of that "make out" I would never know, but I did want to know if it really happened. I realized I had to get my Nancy Drew pants on and figure out how to prove whether the story was true. Then it occurred to me: Audrey kept a diary in her bedroom. Scandalous? Sure. I made no apologies for my methods of acquiring the truth. The only question was how to get the diary.

I drove to her job and told her a phony story about wanting to borrow one of her shirts. Graciously agreeing, she handed me her house key, told me her mom wouldn't be home, and explained where I would find the shirt in her room. So off I went, launching my covert mission. Of course, she had no idea what my true intentions were. As I walked into her room, where clothes were strewn across her bedroom floor and bed, my eyes searched for that diary containing her truths and my fears. I spotted it quickly enough, grabbed it, and left her house.

No, I didn't read it there. I drove home and cracked open that diary like my life depended on it—and there was the truth. Pen to paper, the words bleeding through the pages: "It happened before she and I became friends." Per her words, she felt awful about kissing Sebastian because she liked me as a friend. My heart sank; for the umpteenth time, he'd made me feel like a fool—and now her too.

Once I got my answer, I drove back to her job, placed her diary out of view in the backseat of her car, walked inside to give her back her keys, and told her I had just found out Sebastian cheated on me. With fake concern, she said she'd call me later. My conversation with her was blurry after that. She phoned me later that evening once it occurred to her what and how I had found out.

"Where is it? Where's my diary?" she asked.

"It's in your backseat." The line went dead, and we never spoke again.

After finding out Sebastian cheated on me with Audrey, I immediately ended things with him. It was too much to bear. Their deception left me with a wounded heart and lingering questions: "How could they? What's wrong with me? What did I do wrong? How did I not see it?" and of course "Why am I not enough for him?" as if somehow his infidelity was *my* fault. My friendship with Audrey and my relationship with Sebastian was constantly looping in my mind. Naturally it left me feeling like each of our respective relationships had been a colossal lie. Suddenly Fort Worth wasn't big enough to escape the ever-present reminder of Sebastian and his duplicitous behavior.

In the summer of 2000, I was eighteen years old and again dating Sebastian. After the fall out from Audrey, Sebastian apologized and did what he always did best: manipulated, charmed, and gradually got back on my good side. Once again, I forgave him, but my friendship with Audrey didn't survive. Things between Sebastian and I seemed to be better this time, or better by our standards anyway. Either we were better at communicating, or he was better at hiding things. However, none of it mattered to me anymore; I became indifferent to my relationship with Sebastian and the outcome. The truth was I didn't fully trust him. The nagging suspicion of him being unfaithful was still ever-present and never fully went away.

That summer, my family and I headed to El Paso for a brief weekend trip to celebrate my grandmother's birthday. We'd taken this road trip at least once, maybe even twice, a year since 1989. We had moved from El Paso to Fort Worth when I was a little girl, just shy of my seventh birthday.

The long and daunting drive was a welcome respite. I loved road trips because they brought quiet and calm to my mind and soul. Road trips were peaceful. The never-ending replay of my dad's cassette tape, Juan Gabriel's *Querida*, is ingrained into my childhood memories. My dad refused to leave home without it. It became our road trip anthem.

Approaching Midland, Texas, the intoxicatingly sweet-and-sour smell of crude oil told us we were halfway to El Paso. As we drove further into West Texas, the vastness of the desert landscape only made the faint outline of mountains come closer into view. Traveling past the tepee picnic area off I-10 near Sierra Blanca meant that El Paso was only about an hour away. There are two things my family and I always did, without fail, before arriving to my abuelita's house. One, we'd discuss our timeline about when we'd go and eat at Chico's Tacos—a staple in El Paso and an experience all its own! Two, we'd drive by my aunt and uncle's house, honk our horn to alert them of our arrival, and then keep driving the three blocks to my abuelita's house.

Upon pulling up to her house, wafting in the air was the rich, fragrant blend of culture and tradition. I was instantly transported back to time spent in this city and in Juárez (just across the border) as a young child, riding bikes and playing hide-and-seek in the streets throughout the evening hours with my cousins. Inside, music was playing in the background, booming from the stereo speakers—the slow strumming of guitars, violins, and trumpets of Vicente Fernandez's song "El Rey" (with the occasional drunk uncle singing along of course). As my aunts caught up on the latest gossip, they proudly prepared, cooked, and served whatever delicious Mexican meal they had just spent hours meticulously preparing. My uncles, sitting around in a makeshift circle with a drink or a beer in hand, laughed while they reminisced and told stories about the past and present. Being there was easy and uncomplicated, and time seemed to stand still. Visiting El Paso was like traveling to another place and time. I loved and relished it!

For this trip to El Paso, I'd invited Sebastian to tag along, but unfortunately, he had to work and couldn't join us. My mind always assumed the worst when it came to Sebastian. I wondered if he wanted the weekend to do whatever he wanted with whomever he wanted. To quell my worries, I called his job. They proceeded to tell me that he wasn't working all weekend.

"What?! Did he lie to me again?" I thought.

At that moment, my cousin, Heidi, came to grab me and asked me to come outside. We headed outside arm in arm, only to find my parents, siblings, aunts, uncles, and cousins standing around and forming a circle out front. Not thinking much of it, when my cousin placed me in the center of the circle, I did a double take. To my surprise, I found Sebastian leaning against a car and blending in among the group. "What in the *world* is he doing here?" was all I could think. I was shaking with confusion, excitement, and nervousness. Sebastian walked over to me, grabbed my hand, dropped to one knee, popped open a ring box, and asked for my hand in marriage.

I never saw the proposal coming. I had no idea Sebastian was even considering marriage. Hell, a few weeks earlier I was visiting Galveston with a childhood friend when I met a bartender. By the end of the night, I found myself locking lips with that handsome bartender. If marriage was on the horizon, I wouldn't have been making out with another boy! Sebastian and I'd had casual conversations about one day getting married, but given the current state of our relationship, this was the last thing I ever thought Sebastian would be doing or asking me. However, if he was asking, it must've meant he'd put considerable thought into this. If he was asking, he must be serious! He must be ready and serious about finally settling down and committing. No more cheating, no more other girls, no more sneaking around and lying. This must be how these relationships go. Isn't it? Boy and girl meet, they fall in love, boy cheats, girl forgives boy, boy asks girl to marry him, girl says yes, boy and girl live happily ever after. I didn't know any better, and I convinced myself that this must be the natural progression of how relationships go. I was uncertain, and not wanting to make this an awkward or embarrassing moment for either of us by saying no, I hesitantly smiled, said yes, and hoped for the best.

Yasmin, Eli, my cousins, Sebastian, and I spent that evening by crossing the border into Ciudad Juárez, which—in those days—only required us to yell the word "American" from the car window to the border-patrol agents for them to allow us to cross. We spent the evening drinking, dancing, and laughing at a nightclub. Afterward we stumbled upon a restaurant that was about to close. Our drunken pleas worked, and the owners graciously agreed to remain open for us. They fired up their stoves again and prepared delicious tortas for us. It was an evening I'd never forget.

The wedding date was set: March 2001. I'd be lying if I said I wasn't having doubts about marrying Sebastian. I was secretly looking for any reason *not* to marry him. With our imminent wedding fast approaching, I couldn't help but wonder about Ahmed. I decided to ask Yasmin about his current life status. She informed me that Ahmed was now stationed in North Carolina. He and his girlfriend were expecting their first child together in September. Ahmed had a girlfriend. He was going to be a dad, a family man. He was happy and in a good place. The news sent a jolt of sadness through me. My heart ached for reasons that I couldn't understand. How could I be heartbroken and jealous about losing something that was never mine? I guess I'd never learn what the mysterious "pull" I'd felt was about. I'd never know what he and I could've become. I'd carve out our moment in time and forever hold it dearly.

In the months leading up to our wedding, there had been rumors of Sebastian cheating on me with some girl here and there. To make it worse, one evening, in the spirit of wiping the slate clean and starting fresh before we got married, Sebastian openly admitted to having sex with Lucy, the local tramp. The red flags were all there, God revealing to me that this was *not* the man for me. However, I was hell-bent on proving myself right, and I genuinely believed that marriage could and would change Sebastian: no more philandering, no more lies and excuses, no more other women. I recklessly ignored all the external signs, as well as everything inside of me telling me not to marry him. With all the money our families had invested, I certainly did not want to disappoint them or let everyone down by deciding not to go through with the wedding. Instead, ignoring my gut instincts, I went through with the marriage. I convinced myself that if it didn't work out, then we'd just get divorced. I let the wedding plans resume.

CHAPTER 5

One month. That's how long it took after our nuptials for some girl I didn't know to call my husband's phone and then hang up when I answered. How was I right back here, *again*? I knew I was to blame for being in this position. I had chosen to marry him and to ignore what God was trying to show me. Sebastian was not who I was supposed to be with. As usual, Sebastian had a story for the phone call, and as usual, I let it go and accepted his lies. Having been married in the Catholic Church (at my dad's request) brought a sense of obligation to remain married and make it work, no matter what. Catholic guilt, that's what I call it. So I sucked it up, bottled it all inside, and moved past it like a good wife should. Or so I thought.

Sebastian and I both worked in the service industry. He was a bartender at the local Bennigan's, and I was a waitress at Chili's. While the tips were good, financially we needed to make more money. I'm not sure whose idea it was, but my friend and I decided to apply as waitresses at the local strip club, New Orleans Nights.

I didn't know what to expect, driving up into the semi-full parking lot just after the "lunch rush." Walking up to the main entry doors, I saw the black metal awning that provided somewhat of a distinguished appeal. Pushing through the heavy wooden doors, we politely asked the door girl if we could apply for a waitress job. She kindly called the manager out, and he escorted us through the establishment and seated us at the bar. We were hired immediately, but I was the only one who took the job; my friend didn't have a ride to get to and from the place, so she couldn't take it.

New Orleans Nights was as classy as strip clubs get: it was topless and not fully nude, the food was delicious, and rumor had it that Ian Ziering visited the club whenever he was in town. I found it nothing short of ironic for someone as insecure as I was to work for a business like this—or maybe I was just living up to the stereotype.

I was beyond nervous on the first day. Guilt and shame settled into my spirit, but I brushed them away. This was a job, and I'd make good tips working here. As I walked through the main floor, the smell hit me before anything else. The scent of too much perfume, cologne, and scented lotion hit my nostrils first. Next came the sweet smell of cigars followed by beer, liquor, and cigarette smoke. The ever-lingering aroma of "fake bitches" and lonely men served as a constant reminder that this place was nothing more than an illusion. The techno music blared, the strobe lights flashed, and girls danced and collected bills in their thongs. Such was the norm here.

Walking into the kitchen, I began my training by shadowing another waitress. Once I got past the awkwardness of topless girls walking around for my eight-hour shift, the job itself was easy: get people's orders, get a credit card to keep on file, bring them drinks and food, don't serve alcohol to any underage dancers, don't over-serve a drunk guy or table, and always tab your tables out. Of course, the unspoken rules were to smile, be kind, look pretty—and occasional flirting with the clientele was welcome. One manager even said, "Guys come here to escape their lives, wives, problems, and whatever other bullshit they may be dealing with, so let's show them a good time."

The tips were fucking fantastic, but working there would be my biggest mistake ever and would give me one of my greatest life lessons—in time both would prove to be true. Of course, Sebastian was absolutely on board with my new job and would come to see me as often as possible. It didn't take long for me to find out that he'd visit the club when I wasn't working too. I had no idea this would be the beginning of our unavoidable downfall.

I worked at New Orleans Nights for one year, from 2001 to 2002. At places like this, you were either a waitress, bartender, door girl, house mom, cash-box person, or dancer. I only contemplated door girl and cash-box person, never becoming a dancer. I drew the line there. The things I saw and experienced there taught me a lot about people and life. The people who walked through the doors of that club were people I had known most of my life: neighbors, friends I went to high school with, my brother-in-law (who had *no* idea I worked there), husbands, wives, boyfriends, girlfriends, parents (*not* mine or Sebastian's), and even the Texas Christian University football team and their coaches. There were no real opportunities for me to move up in that place, not to mention the new problems my workplace environment brought into my marriage. Maybe it was the lipstick stains on the collar of Sebastian's shirt that told me that my time there was coming to an end. While working there, my heart began forming a cynical view of life, women, men, love, and marriage. I didn't like who I was becoming nor what I was allowing to enter my heart, mind, soul, and daily life. My faith in everything and everyone was slowly being stripped away and dying off. I no longer recognized my reflection in the mirror. This wasn't who I was, nor was it who God intended me to be. It was time to leave.

By the summer of 2002, Sebastian and I were hanging on by a thread. The constant suspicion about his fidelity was overwhelming, and I'd reached my breaking point. Not sure how else to make him understand, I wrote Sebastian a "Dear John letter" without leaving him. In the letter, I told him how I felt about the status of our marriage and that I was still thinking about Ahmed. Unfortunately, the letter didn't go over well, and we ended up in an explosive fight with no resolution. I needed a night away from Sebastian, so the timing was perfect when Yasmin called to let me know that Eli's brother, friends, and cousins, including Ahmed, would be visiting town. I jumped at the invitation to join them in Dallas for a night of clubbing and dancing. And it was a chance to see Ahmed, even if only for one night.

"Ahmed is back and in town." Hearing her words caused my heart to stop for a moment—the thought of seeing him again literally took my breath away in the best way. I became a giddy schoolgirl again. Trying to give me the rundown quickly, my sister told me he was single again, out of the military, living back in OKC, in school at the University of Oklahoma, and working overnight at Walmart.

"You don't say?"

Sebastian would be working, and I wouldn't dare tell him Ahmed was in town. I looked forward to seeing Ahmed again, wondering incessantly if I'd feel the ping of that mysterious pull again or if too much time had passed. Only one way to find out.

Showing up at Yasmin and Eli's, it didn't take long for my soul to feel his presence. The energy was unavoidable, and my eyes scanned the room to find him. We locked eyes, and with a brief handshake and hasty hello, it became apparent he and I wouldn't be conversing much, if at all, leaving me disheartened. Either way, it was enough for me to know we'd be in the same space, and that made me happy, bringing a smile to my face.

Getting ready at Yasmin's place was always so much fun. Walking into her closet was like walking into Carrie Bradshaw's closet with all the glitz and glamour. Yasmin had the most fashionable clothes and the best makeup, and I loved playing dress-up there! I was always in jeans, T-shirts, and flip-flops, so becoming another version of myself for one night was a beautiful escape. Bring on the high heels, fancy shirts, and sophisticated dress pants! Dressing up always made me feel gorgeous, stylish, and fabulous.

Throughout the evening, Ahmed and I avoided eye contact and each other. Oddly enough, I was scared to make eye contact, fearing I'd feel something for him. Why was that? Ahmed was quiet and kept to himself in the clubs. It was discouraging to know he didn't have anything to say to me, but it was probably safer that way. The evening went by too fast, and I didn't want it to end, or maybe I didn't want to leave him. But, alas, it was time for me to go back home to my dysfunctional reality.

The following day, I called Yasmin to share what I had been feeling the night before around Ahmed. To my delight, she said, "Ahmed said the same thing about you! He didn't want to make eye contact because he didn't want to feel something for you!"

Holy shit! He felt the same way. Which meant the energy between us was still there, undeniable, and he must've felt it too. This time I wasn't going to fight it, brush it off, ignore it, or avoid the feelings I was having for Ahmed.

"Do you want me to give him your number?" Yasmin asked.

"Yes." I instructed her. "Tell him to call in the evenings because that's when Sebastian is at work, and I can talk." And he did; Ahmed called.

CHAPTER 6

It was like time hadn't passed. Finally Ahmed and I caught up on the happenings of the last couple of years. He discussed his time in the military, his plans, his daughter, and his relationship with her mother. We talked about his travels, my marriage, my current job, our families, and life. We laughed, teased each other, and by the end of our conversation, we'd agreed to keep talking in secret, not letting my husband find out. Once our conversation ended, I hung up with a renewed sense of hope that maybe, just maybe, Ahmed and I could be something in the future.

It was mid-October when I saw Ahmed again. The same weekend as the annual Red River Rivalry football game between the University of Texas and the University of Oklahoma. Ahmed and his brother, Malik, drove down for Dallas's weekend game festivities and stayed at Yasmin and Eli's. I managed to sneak away that Saturday night to join them for a night out dancing in Dallas. I was shy, and while I was on the dance floor with Ahmed, he tried to kiss me, but I turned away.

As much as I wanted to, I couldn't risk someone I knew seeing us and finding out about our affair. So, exasperatingly, I burrowed myself into his chest and stayed there until the song was over.

We all piled into Yasmin's two-door Honda Civic at the night's end. I crammed into the backseat with Malik and Ahmed. While he nibbled at my ear, we held onto each other for a bit longer before they dropped me off at home. I soaked it all in. As we pulled into my driveway at 3 a.m., Sebastian was standing in the garage with his friend Jonah. I exited the car, waved bye to them, and leaned into Sebastian's hug. The painful truth was that I was now the cheater, liar, and deceitful spouse. However, this wouldn't stop me from contacting and pursuing a secret relationship with Ahmed. Sebastian never suspected anything, and I'd hide the cell phone bill so he wouldn't see the repeating 405 area code (Oklahoma City) up and down that paper.

Our phone calls were nightly, and I got through my days by looking forward to our evening talks. Email exchanges between Ahmed and I were more frequent than phone calls because they allowed us to communicate during the day. Our mutual feelings for each other were growing stronger, and when I received the following email from Ahmed on November 5, 2002, I knew this thing we felt for each other was unavoidable and was indeed love. Titled "Yeahwellwutever," his email read:

> Hey, there, miss thang. 'Twas very pleasing to hear your voice again after so long, and in standard tonal form as well (glad the "Tussin" worked)! Well, so now I'm guessing things betwixt us-selves are changing, i.e., "one's feelings for another seem to be evolving greatly and with marked significance." So where I would once calculate my rate of affection in thoughts per week, I now must figure my infatuation in thoughts per hour—go ahead and laugh; I'll always

blame whatever on you (please notice that hitherto I've been trying rather desperately to avoid using "like" and that other treacherous, unmentionable, soul-stirring "L" word). Anyway, effective immediately, from now and until further notice, regarding all of my expressed or written remarks or comments concerning my emotional whatchamacallit toward you, I will replace the hideous, overbearing, pulse-quickening "L" word with one of my one less revealing/embarrassing terms: you know that eternally endearing "W" word of mine…whatever! So uh, whatever, and I well whatever and you whatever you know, so I guess whatever darling.

—Ciao, hasta la vista, arrivederci, Semper Fidelis, bye-bye.

Ahmed and I made plans for him to come down for the weekend and stay with Yasmin and Eli. I wasn't sure how I'd get away, but I knew I'd find a way to be there. I loved seeing myself through Ahmed's eyes, but most importantly I loved how I felt around him. I didn't want it to end. There was much uncertainty in my life, but I was sure I didn't want to be without Ahmed. I don't know how, but I needed his presence in my life, and I'd take it any way I could. Right or wrong, justified or not, I was willing and ready to compromise everything for him, including my beliefs, values, morals, and even my marriage. Here and now was the beginning of our love affair. What story could I possibly tell Sebastian that would keep me at my sister's place for an entire weekend? I knew I couldn't keep this up forever, and lying wasn't good either. To my surprise, the opportunity presented itself, and I didn't have to wait long for an excuse to leave. The straw that broke the camel's back was not what you'd think. It wasn't another woman, it wasn't Ahmed, and it wasn't infidelity. It was a car accident.

Throughout our marriage, Sebastian would separate what was his and what was mine. We didn't have a partnership. He would remind me regularly that the one car we owned together was his car. Then, without my knowledge, one afternoon he let his younger brother Nathaniel drive our car. Nathaniel raced it down the highway, ultimately crashing it as a result and totaling our only means of transportation. Initially I was happy and relieved to find out Nathaniel was OK; however, I was enraged knowing that Sebastian didn't tell me and that he would never view me as his partner in life. In that moment of crisis, my selfish nature kicked in, and I seized the opportunity. That moment, right there, was my reason to leave. Furious, I told Sebastian I would be staying at my sister's house to think things over, and I'd be back on Monday to discuss things between us.

The weekend of November 8, 2002 was the same weekend that *8 Mile* was released in movie theaters and was only days after Ahmed's love-affirming email. I arrived at Yasmin and Eli's place that Friday night. Ahmed would drive down the next morning, after his overnight shift at Walmart. I could not contain my excitement. *Finally!*

That Saturday morning I got ready in Yasmin's bathroom, not knowing Ahmed was already there and in the guest bathroom showering. He'd come, again, to see me, and this time I was waiting for him. He walked out of the bedroom clean-shaven and smelling all kinds of good. I smiled and we hugged. This time was different. There was a feeling behind the look, the hug, the smiles. He was intoxicating to look at and to be near. These feelings and emotions went beyond the instant attraction we had felt toward each other all those years ago. They were more than infatuation or lust, greater than "like," and nothing short of love. The magical pull was stronger than ever. Whatever it was, I wanted more of the feeling. With a long embrace, I never wanted him to let go.

Staying with Yasmin and Eli, Ahmed and I didn't have to hide our feelings or affection for each other. The weekend couldn't have gone any better, and I soaked in every minute with him for the short time he was there. All four of us hung out, talking, joking, laughing, reminiscing, and eating. We played a game of drunken Jenga and watched movies. At one point when my parents showed up unexpectedly, Ahmed had to leave and hide out at the local basketball court down the street for what seemed like a couple of hours. Once they left, we all had a good laugh about it. Outside on the balcony in the cool, crisp night air, as I sat on his lap smoking my Marlboro Ultra-Light cigarette, I told him I was going to be leaving Sebastian and asking him for a divorce.

"Good. You should do that for yourself," Ahmed said.

I'm not sure what response I was hoping to hear from him. Maybe "Run away with me, Veronica, because I love you and can't be without you." However, I knew Ahmed was right; I needed to leave Sebastian for myself, not him.

By the end of Saturday night, and after watching the romantic French film *Amélie*, Yasmin and Eli called it a night, turned in, and left Ahmed and me there on the couch, alone once again. It was a sweet, full-circle moment. Standing and steady on my feet, I bravely asked, "I'm ready to go to sleep. Are you going to come to lay down with me?"

"Yeah," he replied and slowly rose off the couch. We strolled into the bedroom together, shutting and locking the door behind us.

How can passion exist without sex? The merging of our souls goes beyond reason, beyond the physical, and into a spiritual connection. The hunger we had for each other was pure, intense, beyond comprehension, and somehow rooted in a love I never knew existed in this world. Ahmed was tender, respectful, and patient. The fire he'd ignited in my soul long ago was set ablaze that evening by his touch. The enigmatic pull I constantly questioned and shunned away was beyond real and was evidenced by the desire I had for him. This was passion unlike anything I'd ever known or experienced. My gut and intuition were *not* wrong, and without a doubt, there had been something between us when we had first met at that car show five years ago. Unknowingly, he had captured my heart then. The feelings I had for him, rising on the inside, couldn't be extinguished by anything or anyone, not even time or distance. Nor did I want them put out. With the solid and deep yearning that I felt toward him, the feelings evoked in his presence, and his showing up at significant moments throughout the past few years, I finally knew what the mysterious pull was. He was sent from God and meant for me. Ahmed was my soulmate.

As much as I wanted to remain in the bubble of that weekend longer, it was time for him to leave and return to his studies at OU and his job. Sadness doesn't begin to describe my heart's achiness at his absence. I didn't know when I'd see him again, but I looked forward eagerly to what the future held for us.

CHAPTER 7

As I sat on our couch across from Sebastian, it felt unfamiliar. The place didn't feel like home anymore, and neither did he. I no longer felt like his wife; this was no longer a marriage. I didn't mince my words or dance around the subject. I blurted it out with ease.

"I want a divorce" rolled off my tongue effortlessly. I'm sure my request surprised him, because he quickly got up and went to the bathroom feeling nauseous. I don't remember arguing about it much or getting much pushback from him, but I do remember explaining why I wanted it. And no, I did not lump Ahmed into those reasons. Deep down, we both knew it was the best thing for us. I gathered a few things and went to stay with my sister until I figured out what my next move would be. The grief over the loss of my marriage would come as a delayed reaction and would eventually creep up later.

On a whim, Ahmed decided he would be back in the Dallas area the following weekend, the same weekend as my mother's birthday. For thirty-six hours, Ahmed would be in Dallas with his dad and stepmom doing some sightseeing, and he asked to see me. I agreed and made plans to drive my sister's car to Dallas after my mom's celebratory birthday dinner Saturday evening at The Keg Steakhouse. Ahmed was back, and I was delighted!

I was ready to take any chance to spend time with him again, especially after the week of self-reflection I'd been having. I took my time showering, shaving, and packing an overnight bag just in case, since maybe this would be *the* weekend. The birthday dinner wasn't moving fast enough, but I enjoyed spending time with my family, so I didn't mind the length of time we'd been there. In light of my divorce revelation, my family had been a great support system for me, and dinners full of laughing, conversation, food, and love were what my heart needed. Seeing Ahmed afterward was only icing on the cake.

Driving into Dallas at night is mesmerizing. The bright city lights aglow in the night sky were my favorite thing about going into the city—the Bank of America Plaza building lit up Gotham green, the luminescence of the ball atop Reunion Tower, and the surrounding buildings with all their lights beaming, drawing you in and bringing Dallas to life. It's a charming evening skyline. Barely able to contain my excitement, I parked at the hotel where Ahmed was staying. Attempting to play it cool, I left my overnight bag in the trunk to avoid appearing too presumptuous. Knocking on his door and seeing him on the other side made all my problems melt away. None of it mattered, not with him. He lifted me off the ground and hugged me tightly. As I breathed him in, I wanted the feeling to go on forever.

"What would you like to drink?" Ahmed asked.

"Miller Lite will be great!"

He tossed me a Miller Lite from the hotel mini fridge and said he wanted to show me something. Confused, I wasn't sure what it could be, but I was up for seeing his surprise for me. Ahmed slowly lifted his chin and head toward the ceiling, only to reveal and expose hickeys across his neck. Hickeys meant a woman had been sucking on his neck. Hickeys said he'd been with another woman since last weekend when he and I were together. Hickeys meant I wasn't the only one in his life. Ahmed never gave me any indications he was seeing other women. So naturally, I thought and assumed I was the only girl he was involved with. In the split second of that moment, I realized he hadn't been honest with me. He had lied to me. My chest tightened, and I froze—my heart crumbled, and my soul shattered. The only thing crossing my mind was "Not Ahmed. Not him too. He wasn't supposed to be like Sebastian. Ahmed was supposed to be different."

What was I to say? What did he want to hear? After all, I was technically still married, but I was always honest with Ahmed each step of the way. He and I hadn't discussed what we were or could be. There was no exclusivity between us. He was free to do what he pleased with whomever, and he certainly didn't owe me an explanation. But none of that made it hurt any less. The room seemed to be getting smaller, the air was getting sucked out, and I was slowly beginning to get hot and suffocate in this room. I had to get out of there as fast as possible before having a complete meltdown.

"OK" was all I could get out.

He explained that the girl didn't mean anything. As if that would take the sting away. Out of habit, I accepted his explanation, and we tried to go on with our night.

Being introduced to his father and stepmother and faking a smile, we exchanged pleasantries about their visit to Dallas. Our visit with them didn't last long, and we graciously made our exit. Before I knew it, we were back in Ahmed's room. "Maybe lying on the bed will help me relax so he won't see the resentment building up inside of me," I thought.

Unfortunately the lack of my returned affection was apparent. Rather than try to keep up the ruse, which was failing miserably, I knew what I had to do. I excused myself and stepped outside to breathe in the fresh air. I quickly dialed Yasmin and told her what happened, to her surprise. She had no idea he was seeing anyone. She was as disappointed as I was and couldn't believe he'd done that to me. Our conversation was quick, and we both agreed I needed to leave and head back to Fort Worth that night. We hung up, and before I went back inside, I mustered up the strength to tell him I'd be leaving. My heart ached, knowing this would be the last time I'd see Ahmed, and a small part of me died on the inside. That night changed everything between us, and I knew we'd never be the same.

"I'm gonna go. It's probably best."

With a heavy sigh of defeat, he said, "OK."

There was no longer a sweet embrace upon leaving. It was different now. I saw him in a different light, and he was no longer the Ahmed from the weekend we had spent together. My goodbye hug was nothing more than a pat on the back. It was cold, impersonal, and full of disappointment, sadness, and disdain—vastly different from the hug I gave him when I had arrived a short while ago.

I jumped into the car and turned the key in the ignition. I hit the gas and got the hell out of there. With tears welling up in my eyes, I called my best friend, Caylee. After telling her what had happened, we agreed I'd meet her at Bennigan's.

I'd driven from Dallas to Fort Worth numerous times, but that was the longest car ride back home ever. I had to put as much distance between Ahmed and me as possible.

The parking lot was packed, but any Saturday night usually was. With the stale-brown building, the copper awning just over the entrance doors, and the Irish-green neon sign beaming high above in the dark sky, Bennigan's was an all-too-familiar bar. Sebastian had worked there as a bartender, and little did I know it would soon become a place of comfort for me, along with alcohol, Sebastian, and other guys. I was way overdressed for the place, but I didn't care. Spotting Caylee sitting at the bar, I walked over, plopped myself down on the barstool next to her, ordered a beer, and let the tears stream down my face. Her words brought me some comfort.

"You're too good for him, and he doesn't deserve you," she said.

Was I? I had cheated on my husband with Ahmed. I wasn't a better person than Ahmed. Before I finished my thought, his name appeared on my phone. "What does he want?" I thought.

"Veronica, I'm sorry. Where are you? Can I come to you?"

"I'm with Caylee, and you don't have to come. You don't even have a car."

"I'll steal my dad's car; I don't care. Please let me come to you so we can talk about this."

Overcome with emotion, I finally said what I'd been thinking all night but had been too scared to speak in person: "You should've warned me and told me about the hickeys before I saw you tonight. You should've at least given me the option to let me choose if I still wanted to come see you, not selfishly choose for me. Why even invite me in the first place?"

"I wanted to see you," he confessed.

Although his revelations pierced my heart with sadness, I secretly appreciated his brutal honesty. Oddly enough, I admired him and held him in high regard. It was because of this that I knew what I had to do. I couldn't let him get close, not anymore. The fear of him hurting me again was unbearable.

"No, don't come. I'll call you later," I reluctantly whispered. Then, finally, I hung up and began drowning my sorrows away with bottles of beer.

CHAPTER 8

In the following weeks, Caylee and I were out *every* night having fun, shooting pool, dancing at clubs, laughing hysterically, meeting new people, flirting, and drinking excessively. By this point, I was drunk dialing both Ahmed and Sebastian. Ahmed would humor me and talk to me, always staying on the phone until I drunkenly passed out.

In the meantime, I was on a secret mission to feel wanted by anyone yet feel absolutely nothing, even if it was only for a night. I decided I'd try this one-night-stand lifestyle and find out what the fuss was all about.

The first guy who showed interest was a friend of Caylee's, Dean. Coincidentally, we first met at Bennigan's. He was pleasant and funny, but he and I never got past our one-night stand.

The second guy was special, Mason. We'd known each other since middle school and I'd had a secret crush on him throughout high school. He was funny, sweet, playful, and had a great sense of humor. I could trust him, and I knew he liked me too. Not to mention he was different from Sebastian and Ahmed. Caylee called Mason and we agreed on a time and place to meet later that evening. It would be the first time I'd see Mason in a long time and although I was smitten with Mason, Ahmed was never far from my thoughts. Just before meeting up with Mason, I drunk dialed Ahmed. For no other reason than just to hear his voice.

As we approached each other in the parking lot of Caylee's apartment complex, Mason cloaked me with his body, wrapped his arms around my neck, and pulled me into a bear-like hug "I've been waiting for this since high school," he said. His words were sweet to my achy soul and exactly what I didn't know I needed to hear.

I threw my arms around his waist, squeezing tightly, and asked, "You liked me in high school? Why didn't you ever say anything?"

"You were always with Sebastian," he shyly replied. I'd had no idea. What and who else had I missed in high school while wasting my time with Sebastian?

Admittedly, I looked forward to my dates with Mason. We went out several times, but sadly our romance was short-lived. I bailed when I learned he was second-guessing being with me out of fear of what Sebastian would think or say. I needed certainty, not doubt. So I was right back where I had started—alone. And being left alone with my thoughts was scary, so I tried my best to avoid it.

Holidays are always the worst when you're alone and without loved ones. A deep ache, emptiness, and solitude make themselves known like never before. I was still on limited but casual speaking terms with Ahmed, and he invited me to join Yasmin and Eli on their trip to OKC for Thanksgiving. As much as I wanted to say yes, I wasn't ready to see Ahmed. The wounds from our last interaction were still fresh, and my bruised ego had already suffered more than enough.

Instead, I opted to stay home with my family and drown my sorrows away with alcohol again, an all-too-familiar taste.

When December rolled around, Caylee and I decided to visit my old stomping ground, New Orleans Nights. There I ran into my old boss, Craig. I was twenty-one. Craig was in his early thirties, tall, handsome, and charming. Despite where he worked, he was kind, respectful, and very much a gentleman. His overwhelming need to fiercely protect the girls who worked there separated him from the other managers. He cared profoundly, and I treasured that about him. He and I went out on a date once. He picked me up at my sister's apartment and took me to a lovely restaurant for dinner. We went out for drinks afterward, and at the end of our date, he walked me to the apartment door, where he kissed me goodnight. The date was perfect, he was perfect, but for me, the kiss was missing something, and I knew exactly what it was. He wasn't Ahmed. Craig and I continued talking. He'd call me at work, and the times I'd see him were when I'd visit him while he was working. I knew he was too good a man for me and, not wanting to drag him into the drama of my life, I quit taking his calls. I gave him no explanation as to why it wasn't going to work out. I felt awful about how I handled it, but I was young and didn't know any better. So what did I do? I opted for the perpetual drowning of my sorrows in alcohol. Not my finest moment.

New Year's Eve 2002 was no different for me than any other night. Caylee and I landed at Red Goose Saloon in downtown Fort Worth in the company of her boyfriend and his friend Dylan. With drinking Miller Lite and doing shots, dancing to Nelly's "Air Force Ones," and doing my best to numb and forget my pain, by the time the clock struck midnight, I was ringing in the New Year by sucking face with Dylan. Outwardly I was faking the smiles and laughs, all while doing my best to put on a brave face. But the truth was, inwardly, I was broken and hurting. To my detriment, my trail of ashes joined me as I entered 2003.

The thing about holidays is that your emotions become heightened. Not only are you feeling lonely, but you become more nostalgic, emotional, and sentimental than usual. I began to long for something intimate and familiar. So I called him, not knowing what to say, how I'd feel, or what I was expecting. Would we talk about the big elephant in the room? What would happen next?

The second he answered the phone was the moment our reconciliation began. We fought through tears, yells, and pointing fingers along the way, but at the end of the day, Sebastian and I were going to work it out. After all, if I was going to make it work with anyone, why not my husband? I owed it to myself to know once and for all if Sebastian and I would work out, and I needed it to be a clean start. That meant I had to cease communication with any guy standing in the way of truly making the marriage work. I called Mason first, and I asked him to please keep our brief romance a secret. Without questioning me, he understood and graciously agreed. I think Craig knew when I quit taking his calls. Ahmed was the last and most dreaded call I had to make because I still had nothing but love for him despite how things had unfolded between us.

"Sebastian and I are getting back together. We're going to try and work things out." The words were difficult to get out, but I did it.

"It feels like I've just been punched in the stomach. I want you to be happy, and if that's with Sebastian, OK." Ahmed exhaled with what sounded like a soft lump in his throat. He wished me luck, we said goodbye, and we didn't speak again.

I cried like never before after that phone call. I felt like I'd just made the worst mistake of my life. The hardest thing about that goodbye was that it didn't feel like our story was over. Letting go of Ahmed was the hardest thing I had ever done. And it would be my biggest regret.

To my dismay, my reconciliation with Sebastian was frowned upon by family and friends. That should've been a red flag, but we ignored it. Adamant to prove to ourselves and to everyone that we knew what we were doing and that our marriage would work, we rented an apartment as a "blank slate" gesture and a sign of new beginnings. However, as it turned out, the only thing our new apartment brought was new problems with old traumas. Our reconciliation would be short-lived and would last only a few months. I was naive to think he would be the same Sebastian I had left months prior. He was just as foolish to think I was the same Veronica who would tolerate his shenanigans. I realized that too much time had passed during our separation and too much damage had occurred. The truth was that neither of us really got over or genuinely forgave the other for the pain we'd inflicted on each other. The phone call and events that followed would end up being the nail in the coffin for our relationship.

***

I'd been at my new full-time eight-to-five job as a receptionist at a CPA's office for a little over six months when he called. I was surprised to hear his voice again on the other end of the phone.

"Thank you for calling American Benefits. This is Veronica. How may I help you?"

"Veronica, it's Craig. How are you?"

I replied, "Hey Craig, I'm good! How are you?"

"Good. I was calling to see how you and Sebastian were doing," he strangely said.

How did he know? And why would he ask or want to know how Sebastian and I were doing? It took me only a split second to realize why Craig called. True to his nature, he was concerned and protecting me. Without saying it, he was telling me he'd seen Sebastian at the club the night before. Unconvincingly, I lied and said we were doing OK. Craig knew I was lying and kindly played along with me. Before ending our call, he wished me the best, and we hung up. Running into an old waitress friend from the club later that day confirmed it. Sebastian had indeed been to the strip club and hidden it from me. "Shit, here we go again," I thought. Nothing had changed. He hadn't changed.

While I had been going through my dark period during our separation, so had he. While I was trying to forget about the love of my life and find love and acceptance in all the wrong places, Sebastian had been coping in his own ways. He was involved in dealing and doing drugs, particularly cocaine. Not only would I find small cocaine packets hidden throughout our apartment, but he was also using. It was a massive point of contention for us.

One evening, Sebastian didn't come home. I called him repeatedly that night and didn't get an answer. I'd soon understand why.

When he arrived home at 7 a.m. the following morning, his eyes glassed over, face flushed and slightly agitated, he couldn't stand being in the same room with me. I knew he was high. We began arguing, and to avoid the fight getting worse, I went to lie down in our bedroom. Before I knew it, Sebastian was kneeling next to me, gently yet forcefully holding his hand to the back of my neck. He eerily whispered into my ear, "I'll do what I want." I knew it was the cocaine talking and not him, but it didn't stop the anger and resentment from rising inside of me.

That was my aha moment. It was the one, the only, and the last time Sebastian put his hands on me in that manner. My eyes opened up: I had tried, he had tried, and we had tried, but in the end, the pain and hurt we caused each other far outweighed our love for one another. Finally relief came over me, knowing without a doubt that it was time to walk away from this toxic relationship for good. Within days, Sebastian had moved out.

CHAPTER 9

By March 2003 Sebastian was out of the apartment, and I was living a quasi-happy life. I'd contacted and paid a divorce attorney to begin the legal process of divorcing Sebastian. As with any stereotypical breakup, I chopped off my long hair and opted for the Reese Witherspoon haircut from *Sweet Home Alabama*, the "Melanie Carmichael." So long old Vero, hello new and improved Veronica.

For the first time ever, I was living on my own, paying bills, and trying to move on from the dumpster fire of the past year. I'd met a lovely guy during a trip to San Antonio that Caylee and I had taken. Nothing serious; he lived out of town and often traveled for work, but he was sweet, and we stayed in touch periodically. And just when I thought I finally had it together, I got some news. Yasmin called to tell me Ahmed had been recalled to the Marines and would be deploying soon. The invasion of Iraq resulted in many reservists being called up to return to active duty and getting shipped off to the beginning of a new war. Ahmed would be leaving soon and going to war. If there was ever a time to speak up, this was it.

I didn't have the courage to call him, so Caylee called the last known number I had for him. First she tried calling him at his grandfather's house, with no luck, but his grandfather kindly gave Caylee Ahmed's cell phone number.

I mustered all the courage I had to be brave enough to call him. I was nervous, unsure how he'd take me calling him or the fact that I even had his number. But in true Ahmed fashion, he diffused the awkwardness with a joke, and after that the conversation flowed easily and frequently. Having him back in my life, talking to him as a friend, revived something inside of me that I didn't even know had been dead and missing. He somehow brought me back to life and made me whole again.

With this second trip to San Antonio with Caylee coming to an end and Ahmed's departure date looming, I finally decided to tell Ahmed how I felt. Once and for all, it was now or never.

I was chatting with him on the phone. He was drunk, and I asked him to be careful.

"Why do you even care about my well-being?" he questioned.

"Because I love you."

The silence on the other end didn't last long before his frustration with me echoed through the phone. With annoyance in his voice, he belted out, "Dammit! Why did you have to say that? I've taken what I felt for you and locked it away!"

"I'm sorry; I had to tell you. You're leaving, and I needed you to know. I won't repeat it, and I'll just let you go now."

"No! Don't hang up! Let's talk about something else."

This was the first time either one of us had said the "L" word regarding how we felt about each other. His response made me immediately regret my decision to declare my love for him. However, Ahmed diffused this excruciatingly embarrassing moment for me, and I appreciated it. He didn't say it back—I love you too. Yet oddly enough, I was at peace with my unrequited love. What mattered more to me was his knowing how I felt. Now he knew.

It was early April 2003, and the day finally arrived. Ahmed was hours away from being shipped away and flown out. But before he left, he called me.

"I'll be in touch as often as possible. I don't know what communication will look like for me, but I'll write as soon as I can. Veronica, don't wait for me. Go live your life and have fun!"

"I *want* to wait for you, and I'll still have fun waiting! I love you and be safe."

"I love you too."

He'd finally said it back.

I'd committed myself—mind, body, and soul—to wait for Ahmed. My heart belonged to him and only him. No way was I going to mess it up this time. To honor my promise to him meant complete and total honesty. I was focusing on getting my life together and staying out of trouble. I was in a total life detox. No Sebastian, no guys, easy on the flirting, no sex, and getting off birth control to help with the whole "not having sex with other guys to pass the time by" thing. Once I knew Ahmed's return date, I'd get back on the pill and be fine. I had time, as Ahmed's projected return date from across the pond was sometime in September. The five-by-seven picture of his smiling face in a frame on my nightstand beside my bed helped ease the twinge I felt in his absence.

To pass the time, I'd played cupid with Ahmed's fraternal twin brother, Malik, and my best friend, Caylee. The two hit it off well. Before I knew it, I was the frequent third wheel to their rendezvous. I had my apartment, and all three of us would spend many nights drinking, hanging out, and taking the occasional road trip to OKC. Not to mention, I was in a good headspace attempting to get my shit together and was no longer trying to numb my pain with alcohol and guys.

Malik and Caylee's relationship evolved quickly; before long, Malik was my roommate. That was a fun story, the boyfriend and his girlfriend's best friend living together. We got some weird and questionable looks, but it was innocent, and I enjoyed the company. It broke up the monotony of my solitude.

May 31, 2003: "Que Paso mi chica rica? What's up, cutie!" read the first email I received from Ahmed. His affectionate terms of endearment always brought a smile to my face. With each email, my eyes were glued to my computer screen, soaking in the words he wrote. I was sowing them into every fiber of my heart and soul. I had a renewed sense of hope for a future with Ahmed.

> Man, it's getting ridiculous how often you're in my thoughts. You make it hard for me to function out here, knowing how much better I feel when I'm around you. So I've decided to make some changes in my personal life. Changes that might help me better perform my duties. I want you to know that I've found another Veronica to sustain me. We go everywhere together; we even sleep together every night. OK, OK, don't laugh, but by some coincidence, I was talking to my M16 rifle the other day, and it just so happens that her name is "Vero" too! It was crazy because I'd met other service rifles before, but they weren't as comfortable as this one. Seriously, you and my M16-mini—you have a lot in common. You're both sleek, beautiful, lightweight, full of poise, easy to talk to, and are both creations to be revered and respected (now, if only you could

fire 30-round clips on single and/or semiautomatic mode). Both of you will see that I make it home safely.

I needed Ahmed to know precisely how I felt and what I wanted.

June 1, 2003:
Ahmed, I want you to know that I am sorry for all I have done to you. If you haven't already, I hope you can find it in your heart to forgive me and give us one more chance. I am tired of wondering what my life would be like with you by my side. I am ready to find out. I want you to know that I miss you very much; I dream about you every night, think about you every day, and love you more as each day passes. You have nothing and nobody to worry about because I am still waiting for *you*!!! You can rest your mind at ease knowing that I am yours 100% if you want me. I pray every night for your safe return home, and I look forward to the day that I can hug you, wrap myself around you, and never let go. Keep your head up, keep smiling, and I will see you soon! I love you!
—Vero

Our email exchange was frequent, several times per week. With each email came more confessions of our love for each other and our hopes for our future. Every word solidified what I'd known and suspected for years and longed to hear.

June 2, 2003:
I've been retardedly in love with you now going on four years; I strongly believe in how we feel around each other. I've certainly never felt the type of passion I have over the past months. I guess

that's it for now. Keep your head up, wear a smile, and know I love you.

—Yours now and always, Ahmed

June 7, 2003:
I love you because of how you seem to shine when I look at you. I see a uniqueness in you that I want all for myself. All I ever wanted was for you to be happy. I've told you before that it doesn't matter if I'm the one you choose to be with *as long as you are happy*. Maybe I'm the right guy for that. I pray I'm the right guy for that. These are questions that could only be answered by our being together. But for what it's worth, I'm terrified of you not liking who I am. You might get to know me inside out and realize that I'm selfish, self-centered, and vain. Personally, I think you deserve better than me. I'll always love you, though. You have no choice about that. Even twenty years from now, if we're not together, we'd still be friends/family que no?...Anyway, what exactly is in my heart will soon be revealed by my actions. You know I've always followed my heart, even though it meant acting on impulse and being brutally honest with myself. Even though I ended up getting punked out, chewed up, spat out, stepped on, shit upon, twisted up, ripped apart, and burned to the ground more times than one man should have to in his lifetime. What I really want is for you to be mine. And please don't fuck with my head anymore. I'm out of Tylenol…

—goodnight darling, sweet dreams

June 7, 2003:
In response to what you want…I am yours!!! I may not know you inside and out, but I have already fallen in love with the man I

have come to know. There is no other man more perfect for me than you. I love you! Take care and see you soon!

—Love always, Vero

June 28, 2003:
You know, some people might think it's rude to invade someone's mind. You need to stop intruding into all my thoughts every day. Every time I think about coming back home, a vision of a smiling you pops into my head! I guess there's nothing I can do to help it though. And don't you worry about not having a sex life. I'll make it all better. Once I get back, you're pretty much done waiting. I don't plan on letting you out of my sight for too long. I just spent the last few minutes looking at the pics you've sent me. You have no idea how much they've helped me to realize that there's still a world out there waiting for me. Tell all the familia that I said hi and I hope it's a great summer for all. And there are so many things I would like to tell you. Just putting them in here doesn't describe or express the emotions themselves fully. Miss you and thank you and love you and always be with you. In time I'll get to show you, so till then, I'll keep typing them.

—Ahmed

July 5, 2003:
Vero darling dearest, I love and miss you terribly. And I can't wait to be back next to you again. I'm sure we'll be seeing fireworks again. Happy 4th, you guys. Drink a cold one for me. All my love

—Ahmed

By mid-July, communication from Ahmed was nonexistent. I tried not to worry and think the worst. I moved back home to my parents' house and kept myself busy with work, spending more time with my family, and the occasional three amigos adventure with Caylee and Malik. Imagine my surprise when Ahmed called to tell me he was stateside again! It was here! He was here! Ahmed purchased my plane ticket for me, and plans were underway to fly me out to Raleigh, North Carolina to spend my twenty-second-birthday weekend with him.

CHAPTER 10

I woke up at 3 a.m. Friday, jumped in the shower, packed the remaining few items I needed before heading to the airport, and had my mom drive me to Dallas Love Field to catch my Southwest flight to Raleigh. The anticipation of seeing him for the first time in nine months, and our first time seeing each other since saying "I love you," made me queasy. The nerve-racking flight lasted two and a half hours, but before I knew it, we'd landed.

Eagerly making my way through the terminal, as I reached the escalators to take me down to baggage claim, I spotted him. He was waiting at the bottom of the escalators, behind a swarm of people, with a broad smile on his clean-shaven face. When I got there, he swooped me off my feet and brought me in for a tight and long embrace. I breathed him in deeply, and with one hug, after nine months, Ahmed was able to revive my soul. Here—like this, with him—was the only place I needed to be. He brought out the best of me in a way that only he could.

He was leaner than the last time I had seen him, and his face had aged in a way that only war can age someone. The smile on his face couldn't hide the dark circles under his eyes or the sadness behind them. Not reading much into it, we gathered my luggage, hopped into the rental car, and headed to our hotel for the weekend. After five years, for the first time, Ahmed and I were alone for an entire weekend. No people, no buffers, just he and I making up for the lost time. And boy, did we make up for it! Don't worry, we were careful.

Walking through downtown Raleigh that evening, I noticed that Ahmed flinched as we turned a corner. He played it off well, and I didn't ask questions—not because I didn't care but because I didn't know what to ask. That evening we spent our time in a piano bar, singing the SpongeBob theme song, playing pool, and drinking. I always had fun with Ahmed; he made it easy. Our time together in Raleigh was laid-back, fun, easygoing, and almost uncomplicated.

Waking me up in the middle of the night came a loud ring from my phone. I looked over at it, and to my shock, appearing on my phone was an all too familiar name and number. Ignoring it repeatedly—answering and quickly hanging up so he'd get the hint—didn't stop the calls from coming. Finally answering, I stepped outside onto the balcony, and I heard crying from the other end with Sebastian saying, "Stop hanging up on me! Nathaniel tried to kill himself with pills and alcohol! We found him on the ground outside my parents' house!"

Nathaniel, Sebastian's brother, had been struggling with a breakup from a girl he deeply loved. My heart stopped for a moment; worry set in for Nathaniel and his well-being. Sebastian and I hadn't spoken much since we split up, and any communication we did have was about the divorce. Although Sebastian had a girlfriend, he called me, which I didn't understand. At this moment, I knew I had to set boundaries with him. Sebastian had to know I was no longer the person he could call or turn to in moments like this.

"I'm sorry to hear about Nathaniel, but I'm in North Carolina right now." With those few words spoken and a brief silence, he *knew* who I was with.

"I see. I'll let you go," Sebastian stoically replied, followed by a dial tone. I learned a few days later that Nathaniel was unsuccessful in his suicide attempt and would be OK.

The remainder of my trip was full of unspoken truths. We never said I love you, and we didn't discuss us. It felt too heavy to bring up. I wanted to keep things lighthearted during our visit. Simultaneously, my departure aligned with the arrival of Ahmed's younger brother, Abdul. At the airport, we snapped a quick pic together with my Kodak disposable camera, said goodbye, and then I jetted back home to Texas.

I wish what followed was the happily-ever-after, fairy-tale ending that our ill-timed relationship deserved. Sadly this was not how our story would end or begin. In the days that followed my return home, I didn't hear much from Ahmed. In our emails, we each had expressed our desire to be together upon his return from war, but it felt like the reality was the opposite. I was left feeling confused. Even with his return home, I was somehow still waiting for him. He became more distant, ignoring my calls and texts, and leaving me with only one option—I had to know where we stood. As the old saying goes, don't ask questions if you're not prepared to hear the answer. By now Ahmed was living back home with his mom, Barb. I picked up the phone and made the dreaded call.

"Ahmed, I need to know where you and I stand," I nervously said. After an awkward silence, he finally answered.

"I...am not committed," He begrudgingly replied.

"I don't understand—you said you wanted to be with me, that you love me, and we'd be together once you got back."

"I did mean all of that, and I still do. But right now, I don't even know where I'll end up. I don't have a job, I'm sleeping in Barb's barn, *when* I sleep, and I'm always drinking. I have to get myself together first."

My heart and soul, once again, were crushed by him. Shattered and broken, I felt that the pain became too much to bear this time. My heart would not recover. Angry and bitter at God, I sank into a deep depression. My mindset became rebellious and turbulent. I became careless and unforgiving. I gave zero fucks about any collateral damages I left in my wake. Love no longer lived within the confines of my heart.

CHAPTER 11

Who knew pleasure and pain were the same? Both are fleeting, stealing the air from my lungs, freezing time, and causing my heart to be still. The only difference between the two is that pleasure is momentary; pain stays with you long after the moment passes.

Returning to my old, mired, and addictive methods of numbing and mending a broken heart, I began drinking again and going out a lot. Guys were back on my radar, and Bennigan's was where the onslaught of poor decision-making would commence. I'd initiate all interactions with the guys I chose to spend time with but never actually have sex with them. I was looking for nothing more than attention and the feeling of being wanted, even if it was only for one night. I tried to forget the one guy my soul ached for.

First came a few days spent with Cooper, Malik's friend. He was a good ol' country boy from Oklahoma: sweet, kind, fun to be around, and very much a gentleman. There was also the lovely fellow I'd met in San Antonio. Coincidentally he was in Dallas when I reached out to him. We met for dinner and drinks, but I left that evening still feeling empty, wanting more, and wanting something real, just not from him. So I called Sebastian.

By this point, Sebastian and I had cleared the air about many issues, and we were on better terms. The new parameters of our friendship had a level of honesty we'd never had in our marriage. There was an assurance in that. We had conversations about our time together and what we had learned, agreeing to disagree on whose fault it was regarding the breakdown of our marriage. And above all, we were friends again, which was vital to me. We were both doing our best to move on and find happiness with others. However, we had a much deeper connection when talking to each other, and it was a nice feeling to have someone to talk to who understood the growing pains of being newly single and in our unique situation. Not many people could relate to a twenty-two-year-old divorcee.

Sebastian and I made plans to hang out "as friends" and meet up at a local pool hall for a mutual friend's birthday celebration. I was nervous about the reception we'd get when people saw us together hanging out again. Although this was our first time together in a social setting, the night went better than I anticipated. Everyone was shocked to see us together, but they were super friendly nonetheless. It was as if no time had passed. We fell into a fun, easygoing, social, and familiar routine. As the evening came to an end, one too many beers and tequila shots later, Sebastian and I were making out in his car and making our way back to his apartment. I made sure we were careful.

Ever since Ahmed and I had fizzled out, Caylee and I didn't hang out as often. She was still dating Ahmed's twin brother, Malik, which made things weird. She was in a committed relationship, and I was not. Our lives were going in different directions, and the frequency of my interactions with Malik and Caylee was far and few between. However, when we did hang out, I didn't particularly appreciate that those around me weren't even comfortable saying Ahmed's name for fear of making it awkward for me. I didn't want anyone to feel like they had to walk on eggshells around me. I sure didn't want them to think of me as some broken, fragile person who couldn't handle even hearing his name. I knew I would have to break the ice with Ahmed to make those around us rest at ease. I was going to have to call him—I knew that.

This time I had an "I don't give a shit" attitude, making the phone call easier. It was a new feeling, better than dread and apprehension. I just had to make sure to stay in this newfound mindset. It was going selfishly well for me, and it was liberating—no need to ruin the merriment I was having.

His phone rang, and it went to voicemail. In jest, I said, "Hey, it's me, Vero. I'm calling to break the ice. No need for it to be awkward for everyone, ha ha! Call me back!"

He called back after a while. There was banter, teasing each other some, making light of the unusual predicament we found ourselves in. After all, our friends and families were all intertwined in our respective daily lives. We knew avoiding each other wasn't practical, realistic, or grown-up. The conversation remained lighthearted and ended with Ahmed mentioning he'd be in town in a couple of weeks. Once again, we agreed to hang out, but family and friends joined this time. I thought to myself, "I can do this."

Knowing I'd be out late most evenings with Ahmed, I arranged to stay with Yasmin and Eli the week he'd be in town. I had time to kill before Ahmed's arrival late Sunday night, so I called Sebastian and invited him out the same evening. There was an unspoken agreement between Sebastian and me. We'd use each other when it was convenient, but not for sex. Well, not after that first night. It was the simplicity of companionship we sought from one another. Brutal, I know, but it worked. The honesty between us was functioning well for me: no strings attached, no complications, and all the benefits. However, there was one topic Sebastian would still squirm about: his nemesis, Ahmed. I didn't care about hurting people's feelings much during those days, so his opinion mattered little to me. Finally, he agreed to meet me, understanding I'd leave once Ahmed called.

We met up at the local pool hall. I could have a drink, unwind, laugh, and chat with Sebastian while shooting pool and waiting for Ahmed to call. We were sitting at the bar for last call when Ahmed texted. Sebastian's expression shifted to that of annoyance. I said thanks, said goodbye, and went to meet Ahmed at Malik and Caylee's apartment.

It'd been over a month since I'd seen Ahmed last, so I won't lie: I was apprehensive about seeing him again. My jilted heart had become well equipped to compartmentalize feelings for men I'd once loved. But I wouldn't allow my infirmities to get the best of me tonight.

It was 2 a.m. when I showed up at the apartment. Walking into the apartment and seeing Ahmed didn't cripple me, so those drinks I'd had with Sebastian must have helped. I'd brought beer, so we all sat on the balcony talking, joking around, and laughing. By 3:30 a.m. I was drunk and tired and unable to drive home. Ahmed offered to drive my car to Yasmin's, with Malik following us.

Walking to my car, we detoured through the pool area. Jokingly I suggested swimming, not meaning it because I was unprepared for it. To my astonishment, and with no time for me to react or remove my phone from my pocket, Ahmed wrapped his arms around me and threw us both into the pool. It was mid-September, the pool water was chilly, and I found myself shivering cold, soaking wet, and with a wet phone.

I was in a drunken stupor, so I wasn't mad. It was fun and playful. The moment was one of the best, most lighthearted moments I had had with him in a long time, and it was one I wouldn't soon forget.

Yasmin and Eli's house was only ten minutes from Malik and Caylee's apartment. Sitting in the car with Ahmed, both of us dripping wet, we laughed about our late-night plunge. After we pulled up to Yasmin's house and got out of the car, Ahmed came to the passenger side to hug me. Standing in front of him, dripping wet, I pathetically asked if he was staying with me or going back with Malik. I don't know what I was more delighted about, him saying yes to staying with me or the obvious fact that we were both thinking the same thing: more time together, alone, could only lead to one thing.

Stumbling into Yasmin and Eli's house, we were greeted by Eli, who came out of their bedroom like an angry father reprimanding his drunk children for waking him, reminding us to keep it down. Ahmed and I laughed as we walked down the hallway to the guest room. Shutting the door behind us, leaving the lights off, and lying down, Ahmed made the first move and kissed me.

Lost and caught up in the moment with no regard for consequences, we were careless, irresponsible, and not careful. Ahmed was different: I trusted him, but more importantly, I loved him deeply. Was this passion, lust, or sexual tension feeding our need to ravage each other? I want to think it was a bit of all three. However, the intensity of our affection toward each other was still there and undeniable. This casual sex thing was anything but simple with Ahmed. The only causal things that applied in this situation were the unwritten rules: no questions asked and no strings attached. My laissez-faire approach was failing me. After a few hours of sleep I woke up, got ready for work, and agreed to see him again soon.

Tuesday evening, as Ahmed and I sat in my truck in the parking lot of Caylee and Malik's apartments, we finally had the most honest conversation we'd ever had in person. To his surprise, I had finally figured him out.

"I was never more than a chase to you, and once you got what you wanted, that was it," I sheepishly acknowledged.

"You're right. I'm sorry for not calling you after everything to let you know I still care. You quit being a challenge for me the weekend Malik and I came down and we all went to Dallas. You still captivate me; I care about you a lot and want to be with you. However, it's not the right time," he admitted. His honesty was admirable, and I respected him for it. Although the truth stung and was not what I wanted to hear, it was refreshing, and I greatly appreciated it. I couldn't be mad at him for it. We were both straightforward, and I couldn't have asked for anything more. On the contrary, I fell in love with him even more, and from the driver's seat, I leaned over to kiss him, and we got lost in the moment.

The rest of the week was the same. We were hanging out, drinking, laughing, joking, and having sex. I relished our time together, no matter how short, and even knowing we were nothing more than each other's momentary convenience while Ahmed was in town. By Friday he was gone, and once again, I found myself sad and empty without him. Rather than sink into old, toxic patterns, I opted to get a second job on the weekends waiting tables at Fox and Hound English Pub to keep me busy and my mind occupied. I was officially working seven days a week. I'd surely stay out of trouble.

CHAPTER 12

Working at Fox and Hound allowed me to continue socializing while meeting new people and making money. Friday and Saturday nights I'd work with the rowdy drunk crowd, and Sunday afternoons with the diehard football fans. I worked with a few familiar faces, including a fellow waiter, James, from my days at Chili's, and an old high school acquaintance, Thea, who ran in some of the same circles I did. On my nights off, I was hanging out with fellow F&H coworkers. James and I would flirt, and we attempted to hang out a couple of times, but our plans always fell through for whatever reason. Thea and I were both single, so we started hanging out, drinking, laughing, and having a good time. On one occasion, Thea and I met up with Sebastian. She even asked me if she could make a move on him. I had zero qualms about it and said, "Go for it!" And after Ahmed's visit, hanging out with Sebastian didn't feel the same anymore. It felt hollow and devoid of any natural substance. I recognized no experience with any guy would ever come close to what Ahmed and I shared. I knew any guy who came along, including Sebastian, would be someone I'd use to pass the time. I would be secretly and subconsciously standing there, silently waiting for Ahmed.

By the end of September, I was going through the motions of daily life—work, home, work, and home again—until one day I got a FedEx letter stating that I was a potential match as a bone marrow donor. In high school I had a friend, Jack, whose sister, Mia, had Leukemia. Jack's family had set up a day to have family and friends get onto the national bone marrow registry in hopes that someone would be a match for Jack's sister. I was seventeen or eighteen when I became part of that registry, but the letter came when I was twenty-two years old. Unfortunately Mia had passed away three years earlier. I had not thought about that list again, at least not until I received the letter. A potential match? What an honor and privilege! With so many questions regarding the process, I called the number on the letter to get more information. The lovely lady told me I was a fifty-fifty match with a seventeen-year-old boy.

I took a few days to research the procedure, read donors' testimonials, and discuss it with my mom. I put myself in that family's shoes and imagined what it would feel like to be the mom of the boy needing a bone marrow transplant. I'd hope someone would do it for my kid. It's funny how God works and puts life into perspective. I was no longer moping over what I thought was the tragic ending of my love life, not when the reality was now a boy fighting for his life. At the end of it all, after a lot of reflection and prayer, the choice was easy to make: yes, I'd proceed with the additional blood tests in hopes of becoming this boy's chance at a longer life. However, the day never came for me to find out whether I was a match. Three days later, my life would change forever, preventing me from moving forward with further testing.

Thursday, October 2, 2003, Yasmin called me while I was working, asking me to swing by her place after work to be there while she took a pregnancy test. Of course, I agreed. It would be my first stop before meeting up with Thea for a little local barhopping fun later that evening. But, as the saying goes, life is what happens when you're busy making other plans. I'm not sure what God was trying to teach me, but this next life lesson stopped me in my tracks.

Yasmin had purchased a two-pack pregnancy test, and for shits and giggles, I agreed to take the second one. Trying to pee quickly onto the stick so I could hurry and get on with my evening plans of drinking and fun, I set the test down, pulled up my pants, washed my hands, and waited with Yasmin in her bedroom. Chatting with Yasmin about the symptoms that had prompted her to take the test made the three-minute wait time go by fast. After the three minutes were up, Yasmin's test showed one line, negative. I could see the disappointment on her face. She and Eli had been trying to conceive but to no avail. In solidarity, I told Yasmin she could read my test because, in my mind, I knew mine would be negative too.

"Oh my God, Vero, you're pregnant!" Yasmin shrieked. Surely she was trying to be funny and lying to get a reaction from me, I just knew it! Then she showed me the test: two pink lines were bright as day. According to this test, I was indeed pregnant. Initially, jumping up and down, Yasmin was more excited for me than I was. Disbelief and shock were my first reactions, followed by bittersweet excitement.

"It's Ahmed's, right? Is Ahmed the father?" Yasmin excitedly questioned.

"Yes, it's Ahmed's," I assuredly replied. After all, he was the last person I'd been with, and we didn't use any protection while he was in town. I couldn't believe I was even having this conversation. My mind began racing, my heart began palpitating, and as the adrenaline hit me, I began shaking nervously. Fear set in. "Holy shit, I'm pregnant."

I began contemplating the last few weeks since Ahmed left. Although I'd picked up birth control pills from Planned Parenthood, I had been waiting to start my period before retaking the pill. My period and cycle had been wonky, so I had been waiting for a normal period before starting birth control. A "normal period cycle," those twenty-eight days since my last period, never came. I had disregarded my tender breasts and the abdominal cramps I'd been experiencing as menstrual cramps and a sign I'd be starting my period soon. The achiness in my lower back meant I'd been overdoing it between working both jobs and not having much time off. I was completely unaware that these were also pregnancy symptoms. Pregnancy never crossed my mind. Why would it? Tons of people have casual, unprotected sex and don't get pregnant. I was no different, or so I thought. I took four more tests to be sure, and they were all positive. Not one showed a negative test result.

"Shit, I'm going to have to call Ahmed," I realized. I hadn't spoken to him since he had left weeks ago. Eli had mentioned that Ahmed was currently in Seattle visiting some girl, and then he'd be moving to DC in the coming weeks to start his new job. What was he going to say? Would Ahmed be mad at me or hate me? Was he going to resent me? Ahmed had no idea his life was about to change too.

On my first attempt to call Ahmed, I left a voicemail asking him to call me back. Impatient and with my nerves still rattled, since Ahmed still hadn't called me ninety minutes later, I texted him. I told him it was urgent to speak with him and to call me back ASAP. Fifteen minutes later, he called me back; there was no sense in beating around the bush.

"Hey…so, I took a pregnancy test, and it came back positive. You're the father, and I'll be going to the doctor tomorrow to find out for sure." His silence was long and deafening.

"I don't know what to say," he finally said, followed by more silence. "Are you serious about this?"

Exasperated at his question, I said, "Yes, I wouldn't make something like this up."

"I need to reevaluate a lot of things, so give me twenty-four hours."

"OK. If I don't hear from you, I'll call to let you know what I find out at the doctor's office."

I'm not sure what I expected him to say or do. However, from there on out, I decided I would take things one day at a time and not worry about anything else. I wanted this baby, and I was happy and excited. God works in mysterious ways, and I knew this baby was a blessing in disguise.

Following up with the doctor the next day, she confirmed what the five other pregnancy tests showed: I was indeed pregnant. The date of conception was when Ahmed and I were together while he was in town visiting in September. My due date would be June 10, 2004. This was happening.

Once I had the confirmation I needed, I texted Ahmed that afternoon, telling him I had gone to the doctor and to call me back. By 10 p.m., I hadn't heard from him. After everything Ahmed and I had been through, was this how it was going to be with him now—ignoring me and not returning my texts or calls? "He'll call me when he's ready," I thought, and he did call the following day. I only cared to know whether Ahmed would be involved in this kid's life.

Summing up our conversation regarding the baby, he said he'd be around when he could, and a part of me was sad for the child I carried. No longer could I worry about my relationship, or lack thereof, with Ahmed. I was going to be a mom, and by the looks and sounds of it, a single mom. Yet I was calm and at peace with the situation because I knew more than ever that God was in control, and everything would be OK. This baby and I would be OK. It was time to tell my family and Sebastian.

It was 5 a.m., and I heard my mom in the kitchen. I walked out of my room, and she saw me, said good morning, and asked if I wanted oatmeal for breakfast. I said yes, and within minutes we were sitting on her bed eating our oatmeal. As we were sitting, watching the local news, and eating, I knew I had to tell her. I kept telling myself, "Just do it, quick and fast, Veronica!"

"I'm pregnant," I hesitantly let out.

As she processed the shock of my words, her simple response was "Aye, Vero. Who's the father?"

"Ahmed's the father," I reassuringly said.

"What are you going to do?" my mom calmly asked.

Shakily but confidently, I replied, "I'm going to keep the baby."

She hugged me and reassured me everything would be OK. No sooner was she done saying it than my dad walked in and asked what was going on.

"I'm pregnant, and Ahmed is the father," I said nervously, waiting for his reply.

"Aye, Vero. You're not even married!" The typical response I expected my overprotective, Catholic, traditional Mexican father to say. Immediately my mom jumped to my defense.

"What does that have to do with anything? You and I weren't married when I discovered I was pregnant with Yasmin."

Miffed at her response, he sucked his teeth, immediately turned on his heels, and left the room. My father's terse response worried me, but I knew he wouldn't be mad forever. It took my dad twenty minutes to calm down before he finally warmed up to the idea of being a grandfather.

Once my news settled into my parents' minds, the questions followed. Briefly I updated them on Ahmed, his plans, and his limited role. My parents supported my decision and offered to help in whatever manner they could. Relief washed over me for the first time in a long time. The only question left was, how would Sebastian take the news?

While I was still married to Sebastian, and before splitting up earlier in the year, I had brought up the conversation about us trying to have kids and start a family. He scoffed and didn't even want to entertain the idea. I wanted to start a family with him for the wrong reasons, hoping it would save our marriage and stop him from his philandering ways. Now, ironically, I found myself in these circumstances: technically still married to Sebastian, but single, pregnant, and starting a family on different terms—on God's terms—with a man I was not even with.

Sebastian was quiet for a moment before asking the question, "Could it be mine?"

"No," I immediately answered. The fact was, Sebastian and I had used protection; Ahmed and I hadn't. The chances of this kid being Sebastian's were slim to none. The obvious answer was no; this baby couldn't be Sebastian's. However, I'd quickly discover I couldn't rule Sebastian out as this kid's father just yet.

CHAPTER 13

Once Sebastian learned of my pregnancy, our complicated relationship morphed overnight. He seemed more sympathetic toward me. He started calling and coming around more. I'd never seen him like this with me, and getting lost with this new side of him, well, we fell into each other's arms for one night.

The following morning, during a quick bathroom break at work, I saw spots of blood after peeing, which, while pregnant, is frightening. My mind raced to miscarriage. I immediately left work early and rushed to the ER with my mom. Unable to answer the doctor's questions honestly with my mother and aunt in the room, I was thankful he recognized my hesitation and kicked them out so he and I could have a more direct conversation. The truth was that I'd had sex with Sebastian the day before. The doctor assured me it was completely normal to have spotting after sexual intercourse during the first few months of pregnancy, due to the sensitivity change within the cervix. Who knew?

Listening to the baby's heartbeat was a huge relief; however, hearing the doctor tell me I was twelve weeks along, not nine like the first doctor I saw had told me, added another layer of drama to an already fucked up and complicated situation. I didn't quite understand how I could get two different dates of conception and two different due dates. It made no sense to me. Shamefully sitting in that room, gathering my belongings to leave, I realized I had to tell everyone my dirty little secret: I'd been slutting around with both Ahmed and Sebastian. What was wrong with me? How did I manage to complicate things this badly? Where did I go wrong?

My mom was the most supportive and my biggest advocate. However, the rest of my family was disappointed. The excitement everyone around me had been showing quickly faded and turned to what felt like pity toward me. Most of my family highly disliked Sebastian because of the breakdown and breakup of our marriage, and the thought of him being the father bothered them greatly. My sister and aunt did their best to be understanding, but I could see through their facade and straight to the slight disdain at either me, the situation, or even both. Eli was mad at me and didn't talk to me the way he once used to. If this was how they felt, I could only imagine what Ahmed and Sebastian would say.

I called Sebastian first. I knew his reply would be gentle and sympathetic.

"So I found out I'm further along than I thought, which puts you as a possibility of being the father."

"I never ruled out the possibility it could be mine. But, of course, I want it to be mine," Sebastian kindly replied.

Ahmed's reply when I told him was vastly different. He was silent and unpleasant. He wasn't unkind, and neither were his words. However,

I could sense that the tone in his voice was filled with irritation and resentment. Maybe it was a relief for him because, once I told Ahmed about Sebastian, I didn't hear from Ahmed again.

Finally, the floodgates opened, and I was forced to feel and deal with everything, including the grief and affliction I'd been avoiding for the last two years. I spent much of my pregnancy crying myself to sleep. Shame, guilt, remorse, anger, sadness, humiliation, and loneliness filled my mind, heart, and soul nightly. No baby's father around to console, help, or reassure me, and no real friends—I was utterly alone and, for the first time, scared. Returning to the one unchanging truth in my life, I started going back to church, praying more, and putting my faith in God. No longer was I trying to control everything in my life. Look where that had gotten me. I was doing my best to enjoy my pregnancy, remain optimistic, and focus on all the good in my life.

The relationship between my mom and me became stronger and closer, and we developed a deeper understanding and appreciation for each other. She was the only one I could count on for genuine support and enthusiasm throughout my pregnancy. I wanted her by my side for it all. When it came time to find out the sex of the baby, my mom was by my side. There was no greater joy than to hear the doctor say, "It's a boy!" I was elated at the news and had a newfound outlook on life with this sweet baby boy. I also learned that Ahmed was again the front-runner to be my baby daddy. As it turns out, my original conception dates from my first sonogram were more accurate than I had thought. However, this time I wouldn't call Ahmed to inform him. By this point he'd written me off and wanted nothing to do with me.

Sebastian moved to Detroit around Thanksgiving of 2003. Even with the distance, he'd call me often. He'd ask how I was doing and how the baby was, and we'd catch up on his new life in Detroit and briefly talk about the possibility of us getting back together if this was his baby. Unfortunately, my selfishness had put Sebastian in a complicated situation. He was doing his best to remain involved and to be there for me in any capacity. He was equally as excited to find out I was having a boy, but when I told him the conception date and due date had changed for the third time, and that Ahmed was more likely the father, we were both heartbroken at the news. Sebastian had stepped up in a way that Ahmed hadn't, and I developed a deep appreciation for his graciousness. But the information about Ahmed changed the dynamic of our relationship, and I didn't blame him. Sebastian withdrew, talks of us getting back together stopped, and our calls became less frequent. There was no certainty in anything until we knew who the father was. We had a long way to go.

As for Ahmed, well, all I knew was what Eli would tell me. Ahmed was traveling a lot for his new job. When he wasn't traveling, he was partying in DC and Georgetown and dating several women. My anger, contempt, and jealousy toward him slowly grew by the day. I did a decent job of ignoring it. However, the profound sadness and deep hurt I felt after everything we'd shared was hard to cope with. The less I thought about him, the less I felt frustration and anger at his handling of the situation. Acting like I didn't exist and like Tristan didn't exist was too much to bear.

Tristan—that was his name, the sweet baby I was carrying; I knew at fourteen, after watching *Legends of the Fall* with Brad Pitt, that I'd be naming my firstborn son Tristan. The sad truth was that I still loved Ahmed. It's the reason the pain was too great to confront. Never in my wildest dreams did I imagine that Ahmed and I would have a kid, much less under these circumstances. Definitely not being apart and holding resentment toward him (or each other), certainly not alone, and damn sure not rooted in anything but love. I wasn't ready to face the actuality of it all.

The remainder of my pregnancy was textbook perfect. I ate healthily and gained the minimum required weight, and the baby grew fast. Tristan was active, and with each one of his movements and kicks, my fears and worries melted away; my heart would jump with excitement, and I'd light up with pure joy—a beautiful reminder of what mattered. It was the best feeling in the world!

My due date of June 4th was fast approaching, and I couldn't wait to finally meet him. My mental state, on the other hand, was a hot mess. I found myself sad and depressed one minute, and excited with anticipation the next minute. There was so much uncertainty in my life. Not only was the issue of "baby daddy" in question, but I also had my pending divorce with Sebastian. The "he loves me; he loves me not" back and forth with Sebastian was exhausting. Adding to that, there was the nonexistent and fleeing Ahmed, my car needed a new transmission, and I had no answers to the million questions I had. With no solid solutions and an uncertain future for Tristan and me, my faith was lacking, and my "finding the silver lining" mentality and attitude were dwindling. My hope for a positive outcome was fading. God was not answering my prayers—or was He?

By early April 2004, I was trying to stay ahead of everything before the baby was born. Knowing that Ahmed often traveled for work, I decided to reach out to him and find out where I could reach him for a paternity test once the baby arrived. It was two weeks later before I heard back from Ahmed. His reply seemed terse, very matter of fact, and without feeling. He was all business, but then again, so was my initial email. He sent well wishes and hopes that the baby and I were doing well. He gave me his contact info, address, and phone number, said he tried to check his email weekly, and that he'd be out of town for a few weeks in June but would keep me updated; and he told me to take care. I cried after reading his email. His response came off as careless, and it hurt deeply. I knew why it hurt, but I refused to acknowledge it as the reason why. As if his email didn't cause enough sadness, I also found out that Caylee and Ahmed's brother Malik were expecting a baby girl in September. She was four and a half months pregnant. What were the odds?

CHAPTER 14

Wednesday, May 19th, was spent like every other day before. Still without a car, I relied on my mom to drive me to and from my new part-time job at the daycare in the afternoons. I was two weeks away from my due date, and aside from being a little more tired than usual, I was feeling great. There was no indication I'd be having this baby any earlier than scheduled. God, however, had other plans for me. Halfway through my shift, I began feeling a great sensation of having to pee. I quickly ran to the bathroom, only to feel the gushing of a waterfall when I started peeing; unlike anything I'd ever experienced before. My water had broken, and ready or not, the time had come. Tristan was coming.

I immediately told my supervisor what had happened and called my mom to pick me up. Within thirty minutes, I was leaving the daycare to head home and gather my belongings before going to the hospital. It was both trepidation and anticipation that caused my adrenaline to spike, and led to the silent and uncontrollable shaking I began having throughout my body. Driving home, I called Sebastian to inform him of the latest development. By this point he was living back in Texas. The moment of truth was near. So much was about to change for so many people. Listening to the sweet and soothing voice in my head telling me to close my eyes, relax, and take deep breaths was the reassurance I needed in knowing that God was with me. In this crucial moment, I knew I was not alone.

Arriving at the hospital around 7 p.m., I'd spend the next fourteen hours in labor. I spoke to Sebastian a few times throughout the evening. He was checking in to see how everything was progressing and to find out if Tristan was there yet. By late evening I opted to begin with Demerol for the pain, which allowed me to get some rest before nausea set in. Dilated to a seven and unable to take the pain, I asked for an epidural. I was thankful for the contraction that came while I was getting the epidural. It allowed me not to focus on the size of the massive needle and the feeling of it entering my back and into my spine. The numbing kicked in quickly and allowed for a more relaxed morning and some conversation with family and hospital staff. On their way to work, my aunt and sister arrived just before it was time to begin pushing.

The doctor kicked everyone out into the waiting room, and all who remained by my bedside were my sweet mama and the kind nurse. Each one of them encouraged me with every contraction and every push. It happened quickly, and twenty minutes and three pushes later, I heard a healthy baby begin to cry. He was here! At 9:45 a.m., Tristan was born. Holding Tristan in my arms for the first time, I thought, "How could every stupid decision I've made in my past lead me to my most extraordinary moment and this incredible feat?" At that moment, as fleeting as it may have felt, I desperately tried to push aside my guilt and shame for bringing this baby into a world where he didn't have a father. Instead, God's peace, mercy, and kindness gushed over me, redirecting my thoughts to the life I had just birthed.

Tristan brought light and warmth back into my heart, soul, and life—something I'd been lacking for a long time. Magically, Tristan's existence saved me. I delighted in Tristan's sweet face, his intoxicating newborn baby smell, and in his presence. I would not allow anything or anyone to steal the joy and love I felt in that moment. I was a mom. It was just the two of us, me and Tristan. My family each took turns holding Tristan. My mom was first, followed by my sister and aunt. My dad and brother showed up later in the morning. The thrill of having the first grandbaby and my first baby was palpable in the delivery room. A new life meant new beginnings. This time I'd try my best to get it right.

After work, Sebastian and his parents stopped by just as he'd said they would the night before. My dad was holding Tristan when Sebastian asked to hold him. Sebastian's smile wasn't enough to hide the emotions on his face and in his eyes: excitement and confusion mixed with joy and a saddening pain. Sebastian's parents were always gracious and compassionate. That extended into the situation we all uncomfortably found ourselves in. They held Tristan, and their smiles and emotions matched Sebastian's. It wasn't until then that I realized how the consequences of my actions rippled into the lives of those around us, well beyond Sebastian, Ahmed, and myself—a painful reality that I'd selfishly not contemplated before.

Unable to wait any longer, Sebastian showed up with a lady the following day. I'd never seen her before, but she was there to administer the paternity test, which was paid for by Sebastian and his parents. Everyone was ready to find out the truth once and for all. After swabbing us, the lady informed us we'd have the results back in one week. Sebastian stuck around to visit after the test was complete. While he was there holding Tristan, my aunt and uncle popped their heads into the room. Once they discovered Sebastian was there, they said they'd come back later. I had my suspicions about why they didn't come into the room, but I never knew, not for sure. Maybe it was better that way.

Once Sebastian was ready to leave, I walked him out, leaving Tristan in the room with my mom. We gave each other a long and drawn-out hug. When I let go, I saw a tear fall down his face. I began to cry, and we said goodbye. I returned to the room, where I broke down, and my mom did her best to hug, comfort, and reassure me everything would be OK. I cried every day after that for the next two weeks.

Every day leading up to the paternity test results, Sebastian would stop by my parents' house to visit Tristan and me. He was holding Tristan the entire time, and watching Sebastian step up as Tristan's potential father warmed my heart and made me want him to be Tristan's dad—so much so that I prayed every night for the results to be in Sebastian's favor. He was there, trying and making an effort to be present. Not an easy task, given the circumstances.

Friday, May 28th, we finally got the paternity results in the mail. As unbearable as it was opening the envelope, the real pain came afterward. Sebastian was not the father. Over the phone, Sebastian and I discussed the results. I was not doing well with the news, and Sebastian didn't take it well either. He said he was hurt and still loved Tristan and me, but he needed time. I apologized, and we hung up. The realization that this would be the end for any future Sebastian and I might have had was life-altering. Devastation and tears consumed me for the next two days. One week later, Sebastian and I decided the best thing would be to move forward with our divorce. Although disappointed and heartbroken, I knew it was the right choice. It was time to close our chapter, move forward, and begin healing. We owed it to ourselves and to each other. Once we knew without a doubt about the paternity results, it was time to get in touch with Tristan's father, Ahmed.

CHAPTER 15

I emailed Ahmed the same day I got the paternity results. Odd how we were right back where we started—communication via email. "One year ago, we were professing our love, hopes, and dreams to one another. Now I can't get him to give me the time of day," I thought. Anyhow, there was no sense in delaying the inevitable.

> Tristan was born on 05/20, and a paternity test was done immediately, and the results came in today. Things don't always turn out the way we plan, but you are the father and Sebastian is not. We can't avoid the inevitable any longer; it is time we discuss the matter at hand. The baby is in great health. I'll wait to hear from you.
> —Veronica

I even attached a few newborn pictures to the email—no sense in beating around the bush. I kept it short, sweet, and to the point. However, I was surprised at his quicker-than-usual four-day-turnaround time to reply. I wasn't expecting to hear from him for at least several weeks.

Congratulations on Tristan's birth! Great pictures! I hope you are excited and doing well. I have been thinking about you and Tristan, and consequently, I feel the need to touch base with you and take a few moments to go over some important details. I believe there are a couple of items for us to consider in light of the paternity issue, not the least momentous of which are things like compatibility of parent-baby blood types (yours, mine, and Tristan's), the term of your pregnancy (I was just practicing math on my calendar here and wondering…), and the inability for my sperm to produce anything male at all. I don't deny even the remotest possibility of my being the father, but I do maintain a slight skepticism under these questionable circumstances. At any rate, these are issues best discussed live. And there are others as well; however better left unmentioned in this writing. So please take these things into consideration (if you haven't already) and give me a call. I should be free this weekend. I look forward to hearing from you!
—My regards to all

"Is he fucking kidding me right now?" I thought. As if I hadn't spent every minute of every day over the previous nine months questioning and considering everything. I would crumble to pieces every time I did, agonizing over my choices and the consequences affecting everybody involved. He had no idea how broken I'd been and how hard I'd been trying to forgive myself while moving on the best I knew how. His subtle accusation of me lying or withholding the truth from him meant he thought I was deceitful. His doubt and distrust of my honesty was the final blow my bruised and battered heart could take from him. He must've never believed in the love and respect I had for him, the love and respect I achingly continued to have. He didn't know me at all, and from his email, he never did.

I called him over the weekend as he had asked, and to no one's surprise, he didn't answer. I left a voicemail, and by Tuesday of the following week, he still hadn't returned my call. My frustrations had reached a boiling point, and I quickly let him know in my follow-up email. His response was "Veronica, thank you for calling last weekend. Don't be frustrated, I'll talk to you this evening (eight-ish your time). Take care."

He finally called, and for the sake of our son, I kept the conversation cordial and superficial, fighting the urge to say all the things I'd kept bottled up inside for the last nine months. It was odd talking with him after so long, and I was stunned when I softened at the sound of his voice. I hated the effect he continued to have on me. I couldn't understand it, and it was infuriating. I wanted to dislike and loathe him, but my anger and bitterness toward him melted when I heard his voice. I was still drawn to him no matter the distance and time apart. Ahmed and I discussed who he needed to call to complete the paternity test. The talk was all business and didn't last long. We agreed to be in touch regarding the test, said our goodbyes, and then hung up.

Trying my best to have some semblance of normalcy, I was attempting to get my life together, move on, and move forward. Over the next few weeks, I did just that. First, I began the process of filing for child support. I emailed Ahmed to let him know of my latest plans, with no reply. "I'll deal with that later," I thought. Next, I got on welfare to make sure I'd be able to feed my kid. It reminded me of my childhood and watching my mom use food stamps to buy food—a humbling moment for me.

I also knew it was time to get Sebastian to sign the divorce papers. It was no easy task to have him sign, but it was long overdue. I drove to his apartment with papers and pen in hand, and I forcefully placed the papers on his dining room table. After a heated argument and being met with hesitation and resistance from Sebastian, I finally got him to sign the divorce papers. I snatched the papers up and walked out. I drove to Yasmin and Eli's, where I sat at their dining room table and began crying. I had failed, our marriage had failed, and it was now over. The painful truth no one tells you is that no matter the situation and circumstances, divorce is brutal. I wouldn't wish it upon my worst enemy.

It was a few weeks later that Sebastian and I finalized our divorce through the court. I didn't cry that time. Instead I smiled, and I felt free. The finality of it all had lifted an enormous weight off my shoulders, and I felt as if I could finally breathe.

After almost one month of not hearing a peep from Ahmed, my irritation toward him grew with each passing day. His handling of our unique situation was disappointing, and it saddened me to see that side of him. His being unwilling and incapable of taking responsibility for his role in it all was beyond annoying. The mama bear in me began to rise and speak up for the child that couldn't. I could no longer let my feelings for him keep me from calling him out. I could no longer stand passively by and continue with niceties.

> What is wrong with you? Are you mad at me? Are you angry that I'm going to seek child support from you? Are you embarrassed or ashamed by the way you have handled this situation? Why have you not called me or responded to my emails? A phone call or a reply to my emails will go a long way, Ahmed. I know you probably have a lot going on in your life, but at some point, you and I do need to discuss Tristan. Whether you want to believe it or not, you and I did conceive a child together, and he is a precious little boy. Do you even care that you have a son? Do you care to know what

he looks like, how he is doing, or how big he is getting? Does he ever cross your mind? He may not carry your last name, but your blood does run through his veins. Ahmed…I am not sure what people have told you about me or about Tristan, I'm not sure what you are thinking or what your plans are, but I am asking you to please call me. If you don't want to talk to me that is fine, but at least write back. We need to straighten everything out for Tristan's sake. As you can see, I have a lot of questions for you, and I am sure you have some for me. Don't be the father that Tristan will grow up to hate. After all these years and everything you and I have been through…please don't make me hate you. I know you are a better person than this. I will wait to hear from you.

—Vero

This was my final plea to him. It had to be. From this point on, there was nothing else I could do but wait. It wasn't long before I received a reply.

I'm upset, enraged, embittered, depressed, and on a certain personal level I feel completely defeated and torn apart inside. I wish it were easy to just pick up the phone and pretend not to feel anything for you. I won't acknowledge Tristan just yet either. The thought of another child I would never be around would really ice it for me. I'll be visiting Malik in late September. Maybe I could stop by for a chat. I'll call you when I learn more.

"*What?* Pretend not to feel anything for me? He still feels something for me," I thought. He still cared, but his actions expressed otherwise. I thought he hated me. How was it possible that Ahmed and I were once again stubbornly feeling the same way about each other at the same time? I couldn't get caught up in his latest confession. He and I had been down that road before, leading to heartache. I had to remain steadfast in my approach to him. I had to put my walls up and compartmentalize my feelings for him. It seemed like the only way I'd be able to get through this. Tristan and his well-being were my first and foremost priority. Financial security for Tristan was of equal importance too. The tragic Shakespearean love story between Ahmed and I was anything but a priority. I had to make sure Ahmed understood that.

> Ahmed, I appreciate your response to my email. Although you may think the situation is awkward, it doesn't have to be. I'm not sure why you think you have to pretend about what you feel; I would prefer you be more forward. Regarding Tristan, the longer you delay in acknowledging him it may become a more awkward situation. The reality is Tristan is your child. I get the impression that you do not want to accept the responsibility of fatherhood. I wasn't ready for the responsibility of being a single mother, but I had to quickly adjust to motherhood. Like the old saying goes, "life is what happens while you're planning for it." I must admit it is not easy, but it is rewarding. I do want you and Tristan to have a steady relationship. I'm not going to stand in the way of that. You have the same rights I do. I hope we can work something out where you can see him on a regular basis. I think it is imperative that we do have that chat while you are in town. I would appreciate a more definite answer so I can make arrangements. I look forward to hearing from you soon.
> —Vero

It worked.

August 26, 2004:

My previous message was a forward one, or at least so I thought. All I was trying to say was that as far as fatherhood and myself are concerned, it's been somewhat like the old saying goes: "one bitten, twice shy." But you're right. It's certainly best to leave awkward emotions out of this whole thing and deal with the issue in a more businesslike sense. The good folks at Identigene tell me that paternity testing using your and Tristan's samples may be conducted only after receiving your approval. You might have to send a letter of consent or the like to the office responsible for this affair. Below is our point of contact information. Call that office when you get the chance, and we'll get me sorted out over here. Anyway, take care of yourselves for now. Tentative current work-leave schedules put me in OKC on the 18th of September. Fort Worth from 20/23. I'll keep y'all in the loop till then.

—Later

"He'll be in town in one month," I thought. "Now, I wait."

CHAPTER 16

The month flew by. Tristan was the best part of my life, and I was finally in a good place. I had enrolled into the local community college and attended night school. My mom would watch Tristan while I was at school and I'd do my homework throughout the day. Between being a full-time single mom and a full-time student, I had zero time to focus on anything or anyone else. Tristan was four months old and getting so big. He was such a happy baby, always smiling and laughing, curious about the world, always listening to every sound, and watching how things move and work. Tristan resembled Ahmed more daily and even shared some facial expressions. He was definitely his father's son. To my surprise, Tristan had a full head of beautiful auburn-colored hair that would shine brightly outside, like the color of a shiny copper penny. I found out the red hair ran on Ahmed's maternal grandmother's side of the family. It was a fun fact I was thankful to learn.

It had been almost one year since the last time I'd seen Ahmed, and the day was fast approaching for us to meet. We'd planned to meet at

Yasmin and Eli's house. They'd be at work, and their house would be empty; I didn't want our first time seeing each other and his first time meeting Tristan to be interrupted by anyone. We agreed to meet early in the afternoon before I had to leave for school. I was nervous, unsure of what to expect or how I'd feel when I saw him again. Memories of happier times between us flooded my mind—back when Ahmed and I were friends, when we'd stay up all night on the phone laughing, joking, and talking about life; back when we simply loved one another. How did we get to this place, treating each other as nothing more than business acquaintances with a transaction to handle?

The doorbell rang, and it snapped me out of my trip down memory lane. Ahmed and Malik were both standing at the door. I hadn't seen Malik in just as long—one year. My friendship with Caylee had ended just before I found out I was pregnant with Tristan. No significant fallout—our lives had been headed in different directions, and we'd grown apart.

Ahmed was there, and it took all my strength to keep it together long enough to get through the visit. I hugged each of them and invited them inside. Ahmed walked in first, followed by Malik. Tristan was in the living room, sitting in his bouncy seat. Walking behind Ahmed, Malik and I exchanged pleasantries, and I watched as Ahmed made his way toward Tristan. He was bracing himself for his first look at Tristan, his son. After several minutes of chatting, Malik mentioned that he had to take care of some things, so he'd give Ahmed and me some time to talk and catch up, and he'd be back.

It was odd to be in the same room with Ahmed again after so long. It felt like we were back in Tammi's living room, awkward and with silence weighing heavy in the room. I had so many questions and things I wanted to say. I wanted to yell, scream, and call him an asshole for staying away, but I also wanted to say "Thanks for finally showing up" and "I love you" because the truth was, I still loved him. However, I knew this visit was not the place or time to unleash the mixture of my mama bear's wrath and love.

After holding Tristan and playing with him for a while, Ahmed sat next to me on the couch. Without hesitation, Ahmed said, "I want us to try and be a family."

His words rattled me, and anger arose in me first, followed by a few deep breaths. "How dare he!" I thought. "Is he serious? Does he know what he's saying or what being a family entails?" His words were what I'd wanted to hear from him for years. Now here we were, under circumstances I never imagined for us. From our past interactions, I knew I couldn't take his words seriously or to heart. I wouldn't repeat that same mistake and read anything into them. Ahmed was all talk and no action. I knew that now. It hurt and pained me, but I knew what to do and say.

"You won't even acknowledge Tristan as your son, so how about we work on getting you the answers you're looking for with the paternity test you want first? Then we can talk."

"OK, fair enough."

Before leaving, Ahmed wrote me a check for a few hundred dollars. It would be the beginning of mending, repairing, and building a new and different relationship between him and me. Once he left, I had a renewed sense of hope he'd be a somewhat involved father, which had been my goal from the beginning of this ordeal.

Ahmed and I would spend the next two months emailing occasionally. I let my guard down a little bit, so we were cordial; my tone was softer and not so formal and businesslike. The paternity test through the attorney general's office was a long process. It was late October when we took the paternity test, and it wasn't until mid-November before we finally got the results he'd been waiting on. We were on the phone when I read him the results. I could feel him holding his breath, and once he got the confirmation he was looking for, he let out a massive sigh of relief. He was even excited at the news. He had a son he never thought he'd be able to have. We hung up, and he called his mom to officially share the news.

I wish I could say this was where Ahmed swept me into his arms and we walked off into the sunset as one big happy family. But, alas, this would not be the case. We'd periodically touch base and check in on each other through email, the occasional phone call, or text. The conversation was always light, hearty, and casual. For now it made sense to keep it that way. I couldn't put stock into anything Ahmed said or promised out of fear of being let down, cast aside, and left alone and brokenhearted again. I continued with my life as if Ahmed weren't involved, and it was around this time that Sebastian reemerged more seriously. He and I had maintained a friendship throughout the last few months. At one point, we had become intimate again. However, once he learned Ahmed was back in my life, becoming an involved father and a potential love interest again, the topic of Sebastian and me getting back together resurfaced. Why now? Was this a relationship I wanted to revisit or even consider again? Maybe it was a coincidence or maybe not, but the simple truth was no, I didn't want a relationship with Sebastian again.

The next time Tristan and I would see Ahmed was after Christmas and just before the New Year. Ahmed was in town visiting Malik, and we spent a few days hanging out. We spent time at Malik and Caylee's with his mom, Barb, chatting, talking, hanging out, and simply spending time together. Ahmed even asked to spend a night alone with Tristan.

So we settled on staying the night at Yasmin and Eli's. Ahmed and Tristan slept in one room, with me sleeping in another room just in case Ahmed or Tristan needed anything.

During this visit, Ahmed once more said he wanted us to be a family and asked me to come to DC with Tristan to visit him after the new year, even offering to pay for my plane ticket and foot the bill and cost of my trip there.

"Holy shit, I think he's serious," I thought.

I kept an open mind and a somewhat open heart to his requests. Did I want to entertain the notion of "us"? It was no longer just me I had to think about; I now had Tristan to consider too. Could it work? You don't casually throw out the phrase "let's be a family." Could this be it? I had so many questions and no answers, but I knew I had to take a leap of faith and trust this new path God was laying before me. "If not now, then when?" I thought. After all, Ahmed was my soulmate and my life's love.

"OK, we can try to be a family, and we'll come to visit you."

I knew I had to tell Sebastian the news. Several days later I'd just arrived home from night school, and while sitting in my car in front of my parents' house, I got a call from Sebastian. He asked how my visit with Ahmed went and I proceeded to tell him what had been decided. His reaction and screaming at me through the phone in a way he never had before caused me to pause. I broke down. Fighting through his anger, frustration, and tears, all I could hear him say to me was, "How could you do this to me again? How could you go back to him after what he did to you? My dad said things between us wouldn't be the same, but they could be better! I can't believe we're back here again, and you're choosing him!"

I felt horrible, but I had to be honest with myself and recognize that I didn't love Sebastian the way I loved Ahmed. I would always want Ahmed. Sebastian deserved better than me. He deserved more than what I had to offer him. Finally, after six years, after all the tears and laughter and the back-and-forth, this revelation was the end of the road for us. This toxic, drama-filled relationship was, at long last, over. Once and for all, the chapter for Sebastian and me was through.

CHAPTER 17

It was winter when Tristan and I flew into Dulles, Virginia. My trip to DC was my first time flying alone with a child. The entire flight was smooth. I had an aisle seat, and Tristan sat in my lap, which meant I couldn't take in the views upon landing, but from what I could see, it was beautiful. The trees were bare, and the dormant grass was a tan-and-brown color. The air was crisp and cold, but it was a welcome change from our mild Texas winters—truly a breath of fresh air. Growing up in Texas, certain seasons are elusive, winter being one of them. So being able to visit and experience a place with a winter full of cold and snow was pure magic.

One year before, I'd had no contact with Ahmed; I'd been pregnant and alone. Yet that day in January 2005, I was walking toward baggage claim at Dulles Airport, looking for Ahmed while carrying our child in my arms. God had a funny way of redirecting my path and always leading me back to Ahmed.

Ahmed found us quickly; before long, we were in his rental car heading back to the apartment he shared with his roommate. It wasn't your typical bachelor pad with beer bottles, empty pizza boxes, and random women's lingerie everywhere. Instead it had nice furniture, it was clean, and it was very much an apartment of young, up-and-coming professionals. I was impressed; Ahmed seemed to be getting his life together. Ahmed's bedroom was toward the back of the apartment—once again, a clean and organized bedroom with a bed big enough for all three of us.

I was nervous about spending the night with Ahmed because I knew how I felt about him, which made me weak around him. My heart melted being near him, and my soul longed to be with him. I got lost in his eyes, kiss, and touch. I became a puddle of mush. However, we were interrupted by the phone call he let go to voicemail. A woman's voice echoed through his answering machine, saying she missed him, loved him, and would talk to him soon. It never occurred to me to ask Ahmed if he was involved with or seeing someone. I should've known better, and that was my mistake. He explained that she was not his girlfriend but someone he had been seeing; it was nothing serious, and she didn't mean anything to him. However, none of it mattered because I knew how he and I felt about each other. My focus was on how we felt about each other now.

We'd spend the next few days doing some sightseeing. Ahmed took the scenic route and drove down Route 193, also known as the Georgetown Pike, to the George Washington Memorial Parkway, all the way into DC. The panoramic views were extraordinary. Tall pine and bare oak trees flanked both sides of the roadway as we drove past Great Falls Park. The closer we got to DC, the more the Potomac River began peeking through the trees. It wasn't long before I saw the famous spires from Healy Hall at Georgetown University across the Potomac River. Then the Washington Monument came into view. The scenery was spectacular, and I felt like the luckiest girl to be there. I fell in love with the history, vibrance, and energy of DC and its surroundings. This place was remarkable, and I didn't want to leave. I didn't want the feeling to end.

My second and last night with Ahmed was unexpected and threw me for a loop. Up until then, Ahmed and I had been enjoying each other's company. He'd been interacting with and getting to know Tristan. Despite the previous night's unpleasantness with the phone call, I was enjoying our time together. I wasn't sure what to call us, but all three of us together felt like a family. That night, after Tristan went to sleep, Ahmed told me he loved me, and to my surprise, I couldn't say it back to him. I'd spent so many nights over the last year aching to hear those words from him. Finally, he was saying the exact words I'd hoped to hear. Words he hadn't said to me since he had deployed overseas two years ago. What did I do? I got scared—fear took over, I froze, and I held back, unable to say the one thing I wanted desperately to say most to him in this world. Saying "I love you" comes from a place of vulnerability, and I wasn't ready to be vulnerable with him or let my guard down. I explained that to him, and he said he understood and was willing to wait.

The next day I don't think either Ahmed or I knew how to act or what to say. Are we, or aren't we? Will we, or won't we? Where do we go from here? I didn't know what the weekend meant or revealed, but I was thankful for it. I packed up my things and Tristan's. Ahmed drove us, in silence, to the airport, walked us in to get our boarding passes, and hugged and kissed us goodbye. Watching him walk away was hard and painful. I didn't know when or if we'd see him again. When I finally got to my gate, I called Ahmed.

"I can't leave without telling you I do love you. I'm scared to say it because of how everything has played out between us, and I'm scared of getting hurt again. But I do love you."

"I love you too, and we'll figure this out."

CHAPTER 18

By February, Ahmed and I were talking regularly, with quasi-serious discussions about Tristan and me moving to Northern Virginia to be with him. However, I still couldn't let my guard down completely. I couldn't get in touch with Ahmed for an entire weekend in February, only to find out later he'd spent it at his friend's apartment to give his roommate and girlfriend privacy for the weekend. I wasn't sure about Ahmed's true intentions, and I wouldn't leave Texas without a commitment to a future with him. I couldn't and wouldn't uproot our lives—mine and Tristan's—for anything less than we deserved. Not to mention I was still in school, the semester wouldn't be over until May, and I wouldn't leave before seeing my brother graduate from high school that same month.

It was mid-March before we'd see Ahmed again. This trip was different from anything I'd ever felt with Ahmed in all the years I'd known him. This time he and I felt like a genuinely legitimate couple.

He flew into Texas for a few days during my spring break. All three of us spent the night at Malik and Caylee's place. The following day, Ahmed, Tristan, and I took a day trip and drove to meet his family in Gainesville for lunch, a great halfway point for all of us. Driving up to Gainesville, with our kid strapped into his car seat in the backseat, me sitting next to Ahmed as he drove—it all felt right. There were discussions about which type of ring cuts I liked for an engagement ring, about me starting the process of mailing our belongings to him, and about what our lives would look like once all three of us were living in Northern Virginia together. Things finally seemed to be falling into place for us. I was absorbing every minute I had with Ahmed. So when his flight back to DC was unexpectedly delayed, I left Tristan with my parents and drove to Ahmed's hotel to spend a few extra hours with him before he left, knowing I wouldn't see him again until Tristan's one-year birthday celebration in May. At long last, for the first time since meeting him at sixteen, it was our time to be together.

The months of April and May were bittersweet. I was tying up loose ends and saying goodbye to friends, including Sebastian. Closing old chapters and eagerly anticipating the beginning of new ones. I was gearing up for a new season in my life and looking forward to the new beginning with Ahmed. I knew my time with my family in Texas was coming to a close. As Ahmed was preparing our apartment for our arrival, I'd seal up and ship out another box to our place in Virginia every couple of weeks. "Our place" had a nice ring to it. However, my heart ached because of the emptiness and the void I knew was coming. Family is everything, and they were everything to me. They held me up when I could not stand, picked me up when I was at my lowest, provided for Tristan and me when I couldn't, and showered me with love and support during the lowest point in my life. Saying goodbye was going to be damn hard. In the meantime, I'd focus on planning Tristan's first birthday party and finishing up the school semester.

Saturday, May 21, 2005, was a celebration weekend I will never forget. Our sweet boy had turned one year old the day before. Surrounded by family, close friends, good food, music, and fun, I was sitting by the fireplace unwinding from the day's craziness. Just as the birthday festivities were wrapping up, Ahmed hollered for everyone's attention. Before I knew it, he was kneeling before me with a ring box held open and a beautiful diamond ring protruding out of it. I'd been suspecting that a proposal was coming, but I didn't know when. Never in my wildest dreams did I think he'd propose at Tristan's first birthday party. It was a lovely surprise. In good humor, Ahmed quoted a line from my favorite movie, *The Notebook*.

"My intentions are completely dishonorable." The words that he proceeded to say next were a blur. I could see him talking, but I couldn't hear him. I'm sure his speech was epic. My mind, unfortunately, decided to shut down after being overcome with pure, joyous emotion and utter shock. Finally, the words I could make out were "I love you" followed by "Will you marry me and make me the happiest man in the world?"

My mind screamed it in my head before I could get the words out. "*Yes!*"

CHAPTER 19

The end of May meant the spring semester at school was over, my brother Marco's high school graduation had come and gone, and the time had come for Tristan and me to leave. The airline tickets for us to join Ahmed in Virginia were purchased for May 31, 2005. Coincidentally, that was exactly two years to the day from the first email Ahmed had sent me from Iraq. However, there are no coincidences. I knew God's hand was all over this and had been from the very beginning. The line "Sometimes I thank God for unanswered prayers" from Garth Brooks's song *Unanswered Prayers* popped into my head. I was so thankful things didn't work out the way I thought I wanted them to. Looking back over the past two years I couldn't believe how much my life had changed and now, here I was, days away from starting my life with Ahmed. God really did work everything, including the ugly parts, for good.

Ahmed and I had made plans regarding what our life in Virginia would look like once we got there. Ahmed would be traveling for work often and for extended periods of time. His work schedule for the foreseeable future would consist of him being home for one month and gone for two months. The thought of me and Tristan being alone in a new city with no family or friends both excited and terrified me. We'd officially be on our own, and I knew I'd have to bide my time and stay busy. We decided I'd spend my summer exploring, getting comfortable, and familiarizing myself with the area. Come August I would enroll for the fall semester at the local community college and enroll Tristan into a daycare near the school. I was ready!

The day was here, and as my parents drove us to the airport, it was the bittersweet moment I'd been dreading for the past two months. It was time to say goodbye. I wouldn't have been able to leave if it weren't for the unwavering love and support they'd showered me with these last two years. I would miss them terribly, but it was time to go start my own family. As I hugged my parents tightly, tears streaming down my face and my mom's, I said thank you for everything and expressed how much I loved them—promising to see them again soon.

During the almost three-hour flight to Northern Virginia, I had a different feeling: no nerves or anxiety, only peace, calm, and excitement for what was to come. The view while landing was also vastly different this time. The sun was bright, the highways were bustling with cars, the trees were luscious green and full of leaves, and the Blue Ridge Mountains indeed looked blue.

Time seemed to slow down from the moment we landed, deplaned, and I put Tristan into his stroller. We got onto the mobile lounge, or people mover as some called it, which would take us from our plane to our gate. Then we finally made our way toward baggage claim—an all too familiar feeling. The full circle moment was finding Ahmed waiting for us within the crowds of people at baggage claim. It was déjà vu all over again. Standing tall with a beaming smile, he hoisted me up, and I felt his arms cascade over me. He embraced us with warm hugs and kisses. Ahmed grabbed our luggage, and we made our way out of Dulles Airport. We loaded up into the new family car (a Dodge Durango) he'd purchased. I was a giddy schoolgirl again with a big smile on my face; I was full of hope and big dreams for our lives together, and eager to begin this new chapter with Ahmed. It was our second chance at getting it right. We had put each other through enough pain and heartache that this time there would be no bullshit drama, no secrets or lies, no surprises. This time was going to be better—*we* were going to be better—because this moment was everything we'd expressed in our emails all those years ago that we wanted. Finally, here we were! All three of us, a family together, finding forward.

Right?

www.ingramcontent.com/pod-product-compliance
Lightning Source LLC
LaVergne TN
LVHW092055060526
838201LV00047B/1397